Kindergarten and ASD

How to Get the Best Possible Experience for Your Child

Margaret Oliver

Jessica Kingsley *Publishers*
London and Philadelphia

The numbered list on p.19 is from Heward, W. L. (2006) *Exceptional Children: An Introduction to Special Education*. Printed and Electronically reproduced by permission of Pearson Education, Inc., New York.

The DSM-5 diagnostic criteria on pp.140–141 is reprinted with permission from the Diagnostic and Statistical Manual of Mental Disorders, Fifth Edition, (Copyright © 2013). American Psychiatric Association. All Rights Reserved.

First published in 2016
by Jessica Kingsley Publishers
73 Collier Street
London N1 9BE, UK
and
400 Market Street, Suite 400
Philadelphia, PA 19106, USA

www.jkp.com

Copyright © Margaret Oliver 2016

Front cover image source: Ingimage.

Library of Congress Cataloging in Publication Data
Names: Oliver, Margaret.
Title: Kindergarten and ASD : how to get the best possible experience for
  your child / Margaret Oliver.
Description: London ; Philadelphia : Jessica Kingsley Publishers, 2015. |
  Includes bibliographical references and index.
Identifiers: LCCN 2015023839 | ISBN 9781784501990 (alk. paper)
Subjects: LCSH: Children with autism spectrum disorders--Education
  (Preschool)--United States. | Autistic children--Education
  (Preschool)--United States. | Kindergarten--Parent participation--United
  States.
Classification: LCC LC4718 .O55 2015 | DDC 371.9--dc23 LC record available at
http://lccn.loc.gov/2015023839

British Library Cataloguing in Publication Data
A CIP catalogue record for this book is available from the British Library

ISBN 978 1 84905 720 2
eISBN 978 1 78450 199 0

Printed and bound in Great Britain

With respect, to all young children with ASD
who are about to begin their formal education,
and to their dedicated parents.

Acknowledgements

I thank my patient husband Don who has supported me in all that I do, especially when sharing company often meant that he read in one room while I studied, created lessons, and typed away in another. I thank my strong son for his perseverance, kindness, and sense of humor that gave me comic relief in times of stress. I couldn't make it through a week without connecting with my sisters Laura and Janet. Don, Son, Laura and Janet—you're my world and I love you!

I thank my editor Kim Fields. How lucky I am to know a genuinely caring, kind human who just happened to be an editor!

Thanks to Lisa Clark, Sarah Hamlin, and Sarah Minty at JKP for being so kind, helpful, and patient as we worked away at the details that go into publishing a book.

And thank you, parents of children with ASD, because I know your concerns, struggles, and joys; and I know that you will guide your children to find their place in the world.

Contents

Introduction

You want your child to have a positive school experience.

The first day of kindergarten! Get out your camera for this next milestone as you release your young one into the world of formal education. Early years, school, adulthood…your child is on the right path.

Kindergarten is a familiar experience. You recall your days—fondly, I hope—as you see your child taking the same step. You know, though, that your child may not respond the way you did. From your child's first years, you've become aware that events for typical children do not always look the same for your son or daughter. Instead of breezing through family outings, your child experiences meltdowns. Playdates produce more anxiety than fun. Birthday and holiday gifts have fallen flat (except for the wrappings!). The typical toddler acts out when he doesn't get his way; the toddler with ASD has long-lasting tantrums that cannot be comforted away. While typical children encounter some difficulty when learning language and socialization skills, the youngster with ASD seems to have a dark cloud of frustration hanging over him. You've learned to expect nontraditional responses to everyday occurrences.

Since your child's diagnosis, you have committed yourself to learn about ASD and how it affects your child. You and your child have come a long way in these first five years. Before you go further, be comforted in knowing that you have shown strength and capabilities when faced with a challenge. Silva and Schalock (2012) indicate that parenting a child with ASD is four times more stressful than parenting a typical child, and twice as stressful as parenting a child with other developmental disabilities. Yes, it really is more difficult, as you suspected.

Take a moment to reflect on your sources of strength: the support of family and friends, the help of professionals, knowledge of facts that replace fear of myths, and, most important, your qualities of dedication, patience, and determination, measured out in heroic proportions. Even if you don't feel like it, you're ready for the next phase.

Transition to kindergarten

Students begin kindergarten with or without preschool experience. Some are reading, most know the basics, while a few have not yet gained measurable skills. No other grade level draws such diverse entrants. Influenced by the trend for increased academic demands, the half-day, mostly play kindergarten program has morphed into a full-day, instruction-rich, please-sit-down program. What a transition for any five-year-old!

Kindergarten readiness asks newcomers to arrive with a bank of skills in several domains:

- *Physical*: a child needs gross and fine motor skills to successfully access the school environment (e.g. independently using stairs and play equipment, fastening clothing, holding a pencil).

- *Social/emotional*: a child is able to interact with peers and adults, take turns, share, wait; has awareness of emotions of self and others.

- *Language*: a child who has a 2,000+ word vocabulary, with the ability to use, categorize, and compare words.

- *Communication*: a child needs to understand and respond to the spoken word and nonverbal cues, and expresses himself effectively.

- *Cognitive*: a child demonstrates awareness of mental processes for memory, judgment, and reasoning.

- *Prior knowledge*: a child has knowledge from experiences that act as a foundation for new learning.

- *Emerging literacy development*: a child shows understanding of holding a book upright, following pages from beginning to end and text from left to right; knows the alphabet, can distinguish a letter from a word.

How wonderful it would be if every child was completely ready for kindergarten, but the newcomers are not generic. "There is no such thing as the average brain," says Todd Rose. "Variability is the rule, not the exception" (2013, p.83). My years of classroom experience confirm the rule of variability with the diversity of personalities and skills my students display. Some students begin the year unable to follow routines or sit for just one minute and have no ability to demonstrate academic knowledge. Others come with a love of letters and numbers, yet struggle with the abstract application of how letters turn into reading comprehension, and numbers create math computations. I've had gigglers, criers, enthusiasts, and hiders, and each showed progress in their kindergarten year.

Parents needn't worry if their child does not meet *all* criteria for kindergarten readiness, especially when they have provided rich opportunities for growth. The educational environment should adjust for children's variability, not vice versa. The most fortunate of kindergartners walk into this ideal educational environment; for the remainder, it comes about through parent/educator partnerships.

The kindergarten year sets the stage for future academic and social success. This important and sometimes downplayed transition is considered a "sensitive period" that influences performance in years to come (Wildenger and McIntyre, 2011). Kindergarten isn't a practice year for the real learning that comes later: the child experiences formal education for the first time and will be influenced by positive or negative events. We as parents and educators need to closely monitor this all-important year.

The purpose of this book

The terrain has changed since you attended elementary school. In addition, you now approach formal education as a parent of a child with ASD. You will be advocating without always understanding the structure of the educational system and its flow of changes due to federal and state mandates, the application of special education laws, and current educational trends. Further, you will see differences in how services are delivered from district to district, building to building, and even teacher to teacher. How do you stay grounded when the ground is shaky?

You are certain of one thing. You want your child to have a positive school experience. Kindergarten is the opening gate to formal education where you will face a learning curve that, along with all of your other responsibilities, will demand your time and thought. Increased knowledge leads to a shortened learning curve. The information in this book will help answer your questions and give you the how-tos you need so that you are the most effective, up-to-speed advocate for your child.

How to use this book

The kindergarten tree has three branches: your child (and the influence of ASD), the school experience, and you. These branches twist together at times, creating hybrid situations that parents and educators may not be expecting. Considering how many permutations this tree could generate, no book is inclusive enough to cover all possibilities. Let's instead focus on the sub-areas that will address most situations and concerns. The chapters in this book cover the following areas:

Your child

To help your child, you and other adults can work to:

- understand cognitive framework and ASD; how it affects learning
- create positive behaviors
- increase language and communication in all settings.

The school experience

Key elements to acquaint yourself with here are:

- kindergarten placement and transition
- academics
- the Individualized Education Plan (IEP)
- communication accommodations
- social and emotional guidelines
- behavior and sensory support.

You (the parent)

As a parent you should also be aware of:

- parent/teacher communication
- planning for the future.

Each chapter supports the kindergarten student with ASD. You can read the entire book in order, or you can select an applicable chapter for specific inquiries. Share it with professionals and educators to help explain your child's needs. For ease of reading, pronoun references to children will generally be *he/him*, and teachers/service providers will be *she/her*. At the end of the book you will find a Practical Tools section which contains a number of resources, all of which can be downloaded from www.jkp.com/catalogue/book/9781849057202 for your personal use.

You have two concerns: that your child is successful in his transition to formal education, and that you are prepared to be his best advocate. Don't forget to find fun along the way!

Kindergarten Transition and Placement

Lay the groundwork, starting a *full year*
before kindergarten begins.

This book exists because I am driven to ensure that kindergarten students with ASD get the best possible start. Without a suitable kindergarten placement and transition, your child and family will suffer the consequences. I've witnessed it and experienced it myself. The eager kindergartner turns into a crier who doesn't want to leave home for school. The parental perks fade one after another... no happy reports of a good day, no watching your child in holiday performances, no friends to bring home for after-school playtime. We have no room for major mistakes during the pivotal kindergarten year. It should begin with the optimum placement for your child along with a transition plan in place.

The choice of "where"

Many parents fret about where their child with special needs will attend kindergarten long before the year arrives. You can capture your disquieting thoughts and make them work in your favor with the help of a profile questionnaire, included in the Practical Tools section, to inform kindergarten placement. First, let's look at the possibilities:

- homeschool
- private school
  - for all students
  - for students with disabilities
- charter school (a public school)
- local public school
  - general education classroom
  - general education classroom with an aide for the child
  - general education classroom with small group instruction provided by an intervention specialist
  - self-contained classroom
    - for multiple disabilities
    - for autism.

You might be overwhelmed as you consider the possibilities when you're in the decision-making process, weighing what you know and seeking the undiscovered. If you've identified placements from each prior category, or searched to learn that some categories do not exist in your area, you can be assured that you're on the right path. Next, let's consider "where" from two angles: the law and the child's needs. I am making the assumption that your child is eligible for special education services due to developmental delays or ASD.

Placement: IDEA

Parent advocacy movements influenced the creation of legislation that eventually led to the current law, IDEA. You can view the entire law and related information on the U.S. Department of Education's website (http://idea.ed.gov). Heward (2006, pp.19–21) denotes the comprehensive law's six major principles:

1. *Zero reject.* All children with disabilities are eligible for public education regardless of their disability.

2. *Nondiscriminatory identification and evaluation.* The schools must use multifactored evaluations that do not discriminate on the basis of the child's race, culture, or native language.

3. *Free, appropriate public education (FAPE).* The child is provided an appropriate education at the public's expense. The child will have an IEP.

4. *Least restrictive environment (LRE).* The placement should be determined from a continuum of services that best suits the child that begins with being educated with nondisabled peers, to being placed in a separate classroom only when he cannot receive appropriate services in a general education classroom with interventions.

5. *Due process safeguards.* A child cannot be placed into or out of special education services without the consent of the parent. Parents have a right to due process hearings when IDEA-related disagreements cannot be resolved.

6. *Parent and student participation and shared decision making.* Collaboration is mandated between schools, parents, and students for special education services.[1]

---

1   This list has been reproduced with permission from Pearson Education, Inc., New York.

FAPE and LRE

As you consider your child's kindergarten placement, the principles of FAPE and LRE come into play. IDEA doesn't tell us what they look like for your child's school choice, and parents and administration can sometimes tangle over the application of these principles because of ambiguity. How do you define "appropriate" when considering FAPE? When are you sure you've reached the "least restrictive" point? IDEA trusts the IEP team to make these determinations.

Let's break down FAPE. "Free" means free to the parents; the public pays for the education. "Appropriate" can have as many definitions as it has participants in special education! The IEP abridges the definition of "appropriate" by putting the focus on the unique needs of the child with a disability. You measure the appropriateness of the child's education through the implementation of the IEP created by the team. "Appropriate" does not mean "the best." I've seen unfortunate struggles when parents expected more than appropriate. All of us would enjoy a fully-loaded Humvee, but, in reality, a four-door sedan in excellent working condition will get us to where we need to go all the same. FAPE tells you to advocate for the sedan, not the Humvee.

"Public education" sounds straightforward, but it comes with a nuance. Public schools are required to adhere to IDEA and its mandates. Private schools are not held to IDEA standards to the same degree, and charter schools may not accept all students with disabilities because of lottery selection. The "public education" portion of FAPE loses clarity for private and charter schools in certain realms, and parents need to take this into consideration if selecting a setting other than the local public school district.

Imagine your child being refused access to your public school system because of a disability. LRE promises that this will not happen even though it was a common practice before IDEA and its precursor laws. LRE is a continuum that begins with special needs children being educated with their nondisabled peers while being provided with the necessary interventions and supports to be successful. The IEP team may determine that the LRE is in a different setting—a separate classroom without typical peers, a building other than the local school, or even a program outside the district—because that setting provides the appropriate learning environment for that specific child. IDEA requires the public school to cover the cost of an alternative program if the school district needs to enroll the child elsewhere. However, parents cannot independently select a private institution and then ask the school district to pay for the program. You want the involvement of the team to choose the best fit for your child whether it is with typical peers, in a self-contained classroom, or a program outside the district.

For homeschoolers, the funding of IDEA services is determined at the state level. You will need to check with your state to learn how IDEA is implemented for the homeschooled child. If you are considering this placement for your child, I recommend the book, *Homeschooling the Child with Autism: Answers to the Top Questions Parents and Professionals Ask*, by Patricia Schetter (2009).

Placement: the child's needs

In the waltz of making a school choice, the parent begins the dance with the local school's special education administrator, until the charter school taps you on the shoulder to present its commercial. Next you hear grandma say, "May I have this dance?" as she gives her opinion. Look at all these people on the school-choice dance floor! While you are being lured by convenient school hours, a phenomenal sensory room, or the most current technology, your child's specific needs sit on a chair against the wall of the dance floor, forgotten for the moment. Sometimes the amount of school choice information can be so overwhelming that you find it difficult to measure your child's needs against school options. Perhaps you will experience the opposite with underwhelming choices. You need a focal point—an anchor—as you search.

The crafters of IDEA offer you their wisdom through FAPE. "Appropriate" defines itself as the implementation of the IEP that captures the *child's unique needs.* You may not know all the facts or pitfalls about school choices, but you know what your child needs. You have only one question to ask yourself as you sort through the information you learn in your search: "Is this what my child needs?" Your focus is on selecting a program that best matches your child's needs while turning a blind eye to all the lights, gadgets, and conveniences that don't answer the question.

Addressing communication, socialization, and behavior ■
I worried, as have the parents of students I taught, about our children's communication, socialization, and behaviors. When students are provided with the right supports, academics fall into place. When I meet parents for kindergarten interviews, I ask them to tell me about their child. I'm mentally counting how many topics we cover, or minutes that pass, before academics is mentioned (at least three topics and at least five minutes, on average). When the parents do discuss academics, they express it as if it was atonement for other challenging behaviors. "But he's really smart! He knew his alphabet before he was two, and he's reading words." What irony when we realize that academics may not be the most important item in our school search.

Because ASD presents with communication, socialization, and behavioral challenges that are especially notable in younger children, we need to know what supports are offered in these areas. For every program you consider, ask if the team writes IEP goals for communication, socialization, and behaviors. Have the representative explain to you how these challenges are supported in daily activities, not just specific IEP goals. Find out how the school provides speech and occupational therapies. Do they have in-house therapists or do they hire contracted therapists, and how often do they provide services? Do they have access to a behavioral consultant? FAPE requires that the school serves your child and his disability appropriately by meeting his unique needs. Let your prospective educators know that your child's unique needs include support for communication, socialization, and behavior—and, remember to be specific.

Academic considerations

I don't mean to downplay academics. Please see Chapter 4 for an in-depth look at what is taught in kindergarten and how the lessons can be tailored to suit the child with ASD. Keep in mind that IDEA mandates are 100 percent enforced in public schools, but not to that degree for private and charter schools. Academically, this means that public school educators must meet requirements to be what IDEA calls a *highly qualified teacher* for all subjects taught. Private schools are not held to this requirement. Teacher certification and highly-qualified requirements in charter schools vary from state to state. Some states require that only a percentage, or none, of their teachers possess these qualifications. If you are considering a private or charter school, ask about the qualifications of their teachers.

If you choose your local public school and consider no other options, you will need to find your child's place on the educational continuum: general education with supports, self-contained classroom, or program in a separate building. The mantra stands: "Is this what my child needs?" FAPE was made precisely for this situation.

Charter schools, which are public schools, may not have the entire continuum of educational settings, but should be flexible in meeting the child's unique needs. Because of the variety among charter schools, verify that the one you are interested in has the resources necessary to meet your child's educational needs.

Revisiting the IDEA principles

Let's look again at the six IDEA principles, this time with your child's needs in mind:

1. *Zero reject.* All children with disabilities are eligible for public education regardless of their disability. *Rejection happened in the dark ages! IDEA protects your child.*

2. *Nondiscriminatory identification and evaluation.* The schools must use multifactored evaluations that do not discriminate on the basis of the child's race, culture, or native language. *Was your child evaluated for special education services prior to the start of kindergarten? If not, please contact your local public school to request the evaluation. Homeschoolers, you're also eligible.*

3. *Free, appropriate public education (FAPE).* The child is provided an appropriate education at the public's expense. The child will have an IEP. *FAPE is influencing your school search. The emphasis on "appropriate" is realized through the IEP where the child's unique needs are emphasized. You search for a school by asking, "Is this what my child needs?"*

4. *Least restrictive environment (LRE).* The placement should be determined from a continuum of services that best suits the child that begins with being educated with nondisabled peers, to being placed in a separate classroom only when he cannot receive appropriate services in a general education classroom with interventions. *Your child should have a thoughtful placement for kindergarten created by a team, not prescribed by an administrator.*

5. *Due process safeguards.* A child cannot be placed into or out of special education services without the consent of the parent. Parents have a right to due process hearings when IDEA-related disagreements cannot be resolved. *Be assured that IDEA has procedures to resolve conflicts, including the decision about where your child will be educated.*

6. *Parent and student participation and shared decision making.* Collaboration is mandated between schools, parents, and students for special education services. *How else is everyone going to understand your child?*

Your child is dependent on you to meet his unique needs in this crucial transition to formal education. Continue with your steadfast dedication and teamwork that assures the best path forward.

Profile questionnaire

The pencil meets the paper to help clarify your child's profile for kindergarten placement. Part I of the Profile Questionnaire (in the Practical Tools section at the back of the book) asks you to indicate the level of support your child needs for common kindergarten skills, and Part II of the Profile Questionnaire prompts you to fill in the blanks. Writing causes us to reflect, and reflection is a necessary part of learning. When you've completed Part II, you may be surprised that you learned something new about your child's strengths and interests or that you are growing as an advocate. Expect this writing assignment to expand your knowledge and confidence—a nice byproduct as you help prepare your child for kindergarten!

The Profile Questionnaire does its job if you alone fill it out. However, for a richer profile, you can ask other professionals and educators to do the same. If everyone's input is relatively identical, your answers are confirmed. If your profile differs from the preschool teacher's or the speech therapist's, you have an indication that your child responds differently to a variety of environments. I have seen both extremes as a teacher: I get the child's best behavior and they are worn out and cranky when they go home, or my student is learning how to be in school while expressing a desire not to be there and is more comfortable at home.

If your child is currently receiving special education services, share the completed profile with the IEP team. Provide copies to the representatives of all prospective school choices. Your investment in time will pay off as you use the Profile Questionnaire to communicate your child's needs.

Transition plan

The early years are coming to a close as your child approaches the next milestone. Forest and colleagues (2004, p.103–112) note, "The transition of young children with ASD from preschool to kindergarten is an important event both for sustaining gains made during preschool and for establishing future social and academic development." We want our kindergartners to continue gaining ground both academically and socially, and that's why the transition planning is so important. Kindergarten is not a practice year; no other year will compare in terms of laying the foundation for how your child will perform well into high school.

The Transition Timeline (see Practical Tools section) will help you organize the important steps toward a smooth entry into kindergarten that, in turn, will support your child's success. It starts you off a year in advance, but be aware that some private schools may require pre-registration more than a year before kindergarten begins, and act accordingly.

Transitional IEP

Children who attend preschool and receive special education services have a transitional IEP created in the spring prior to kindergarten. Parents, please be aware that you may be asked by a school representative or teacher to remove your child from special education services and the IEP at this meeting. Perhaps the team suggests a 504 plan instead (Section 504 of the Americans with Disabilities Act), or suggests that your child is ready to enter kindergarten with no additional supports. This may occur because your child was successful in preschool and showed continual gains. I urge you to keep the IEP intact for the kindergarten year regardless of the current level of success. Your child's preschool teacher may have created an ideal situation for growth and your child responded well. This gives you no guarantee that kindergarten will be the same.

Your child will:

- be in a new setting

- be among different and more peers

- have a new teacher

- have to learn new classroom routines

- have expectations for increased independence

- experience abstract concepts in academics

- be expected to carry forward and generalize preschool learning.

We're asking a lot from our kindergartner, so we should be giving a lot of support in return. In *every* case I observed where a child had preschool special education services, and then had the support removed in kindergarten, the child did not transition successfully. Keep the IEP and the special education services. In the spring of your child's kindergarten year, you can reconsider if the team believes your child no longer needs support. IDEA backs you, too, with its *due process safeguards* that require parental consent to remove a student from special education services.

The Profile Questionnaire and Transition Timeline will organize your responsibilities as you prepare your child for kindergarten. Wouldn't we be super-advocates if we could plan away all the challenges our children might experience? Instead, we level the playing field where we can, and we teach our children flexibility when the world does not bend their way. Onward, parents, onward!

Parent/Teacher Communication

Agree on a communication plan as soon as possible!

Your child has communication deficits, so how will he advocate for himself throughout the school day, and how will he let you know about his needs at school? If you establish effective parent/teacher communication practices now, you can avoid potential problems and make fast work out of the glitches that will occur.

Plan to communicate

The *pre* in *preschool* foretells that school is about to happen. It's not a continuum: your child will take a large leap to go from preschool to kindergarten. If you've never had a child with special needs enter kindergarten, you lack experience and understanding of some things to come. Parents need a more refined skill set to advocate for their children once formal education begins, yet they have no road map or training to prepare for the next step. Parent/teacher communication will light the path as your child transitions to kindergarten, and the remainder of this book will inform you of the terrain.

We're three on a tree: the child, the parents, and the school experience. Your child's teacher is the portal to all things school, and the co-creator of many tree branches. Until I became a teacher, I didn't comprehend the depth of work and responsibility required to get the job done. I explained to my accountant friend that teaching is like having two jobs, and not just during tax season. Each evening and weekend, I would prepare the script and props, and each day I would stage the learning play. The job of teaching often appears in "Top 10" lists of stressful professions. Williams and Poel (2006) found that special educators leave the field in greater numbers than general educators because of stress. This is your teacher's world where the growth of each student is her top priority. Who better to understand the stress of parenting a child with special needs than the educator who experiences the stress in a different arena? The parent/teacher relationship calls for understanding and support. We need each other.

Research shows that student success increases as the collaboration between parents and teachers increases (Ginsberg, 2012; Hughes and Read, 2012). While this relationship may occur naturally, the federal law IDEA mandates the participation of your child's teacher, along with a team of professionals that can include other teachers: speech, occupational, and physical therapists; principals; and district representatives. You have a layer added to your parenting responsibilities because of IDEA and its product, the IEP. Because of IDEA's gravitas, the IEP can parade as the big deal in your child's first year in formal education. Don't let it. Keep going back to the parent/teacher relationship—good communication is the fundamental big deal. Access to the team begins with the teacher. Regular parent/teacher communication builds the relationship that supports ongoing student success. It keeps drama (a.k.a. stress) at a minimum and creates trust among team members.

Parent/teacher communication can be as individual as the child, yet core requisites need to be met. The relationship can be built intentionally, regardless of the starting point with your child's new teacher. In this information age, we can tap into multiple communication options. However, the best plan is to *have a plan*!

Communication traits

Let's first consider the different communication traits a parent or teacher may possess. We have probably acted within each of the following categories given differing circumstances, and may identify ourselves or a teacher in one of them, especially before we have a communication plan in place.

Nonresponsive communication style

We know how frustrated we feel when we're ignored, especially when we are tending to an urgent matter. When we do connect, we're discouraged if the communication is cut short. Nonresponsive communication creates frustration instead of cooperation.

A nonresponsive parent:

- doesn't pick up when they see school on caller ID
- doesn't remove handouts from the student's backpack
- needs several reminders for signatures on forms.

A nonresponsive teacher:

- isn't available for phone conversations
- doesn't answer emails from parents
- is short and evasive when connection is made.

Unstructured communication style

The unstructured communicator could be overwhelmed with responsibilities and miss the details that promote daily upkeep; or, they could live by the motto, "Let well enough alone." Regardless, the unstructured communicator is at risk of becoming the invisible member of the IEP team.

An unstructured communicator parent:

- takes care of needs as they arise; otherwise, they are not heard from

- doesn't always remember to share pertinent information about their child.

An unstructured communicator teacher:

- isn't an initiator

- contacts the parent only when something goes wrong.

Overwhelming communication style

We need to distinguish between temporary and generalized overwhelming communication. As a parent and teacher, I've experienced spurts of brisk back-and-forth communication that was necessary to resolve an urgent matter. But when a parent or teacher leaves you feeling overwhelmed with voluminous communication on a regular basis, you're dealing with the *generalized* version.

An overwhelming communicator parent:

- sends lengthy, unedited emails several times a week

- calls school office during class time and demands to speak with the teacher

- doesn't allow enough time for the teacher to respond to requests

- talks to everyone but the teacher (administrators, program coordinator) about their concerns.

An overwhelming communicator teacher:

- contacts the child's parents for minor infractions

- leaves the parent feeling as if she is the cause of the problem or should be the one to find a solution

- wants signatures on documents that have not been explained.

Communication guidelines

When we have a plan in place, we reduce our stress and the temptation to fall into one of the communication traits previously listed. Every good plan has guidelines. Consider these best practices for parent/teacher communication.

Daily exchanges

As a parent, best practice is to:

- communicate as if your child was the most important student in the school—he is!

- learn the teacher's mode of daily communication and ask for modification if the current method isn't effective

- remain active and involved in your child's daily school life.

As a teacher, best practice is to:

- communicate for a child who can't always speak for himself

- schedule time (and keep it sacred) for preparing regular communication to the parent

- include endearing information about the child's day

- communicate vigorously even when the parent is not involved.

Exceptional circumstances

For the parent, these include:

- letting the teacher know about your child's new growth or challenges

- if you wonder if something is worth communicating to the teacher, it most likely will be helpful information.

For the teacher, these include:

- calling or writing a note about *positive* events

- communicating difficult information by staying with the facts and withholding opinion.

Conflict resolution

As a parent, make sure you:

- communicate for information, not confrontation
- consider writing your position on an issue as a way of clarifying your thoughts
- stay with an issue until it's resolved to your satisfaction
- take a day to consider alternatives suggested by other team members before accepting or rejecting
- make your best effort to be a team member; consider using the services of an advocate or mediator.

A teacher should ensure they:

- communicate for information, not confrontation
- use data to support the students' abilities
- rely on the IEP team to help resolve conflicts
- remind yourself that you are part of a team that is working for the benefit of the student; it's not an "us against them" mentality.

Making the plan

You need two forms, a ten-minute meeting with the teacher, and signatures. That's all! You now have a communication plan in place for the entire school year. The more informal of us may prefer to rely on good faith and magic for effective communication. However, everyone does better when the parameters are agreed upon and sealed with signatures.

When do you set the plan in place? Ideally, you will have the agreement completed before the first day of school. You can take the forms to orientation or open house; or you can create your own opportunity by visiting the school/teacher before day one. However, the promise of effective communication is always available. If you missed the chance to get the plan in place before school began, you can implement it at any time.

Just two forms

The forms convey all facts and no feelings. The end product is a plan that works for everyone, regardless of personality differences. You might bond immediately with your child's teacher, or you may sense distance and awkwardness. That doesn't change the fact that we, the teacher and the parents, are in this together for the entire year. We don't need warm feelings and long walks around the playground to make the relationship viable. We have workable facts.

Parent/teacher communication checklist (in Practical Tools section)

You and the teacher respond to the same checklist in three categories:

- *Communication method/style* (Which methods do I use to communicate? What communication style do I prefer?)

- *Frequency* (How often do I prefer to communicate?)

- *Availability* (When am I able to talk?)

You can have your portion filled out in advance, or you can complete the form in tandem with your child's teacher. The information gleaned from this checklist informs the agreement between parents and teachers.

Individualized communication plan (in Practical Tools section)

Upon completion, you and the teacher have agreed upon a communication plan: which method(s)/style(s), what times, frequency, and availability. The form captures the elusive contact information for both parties. You may not realize how valuable this component is! Advocacy can be thwarted at its inception due to outdated or no contact information. The individualized communication plan is the gateway to collaboration with student success as its purpose.

The power of the plan

In my first years as a special educator, I scrambled to make certain that the parents of my students were fully informed about their child's day. Through my efforts, I learned the variety of communication styles of the parents. Some enjoyed relaxing chats that could last up to an hour; others just wanted quick text messages. My students' parents taught me how to accommodate all styles.

Some teachers outline their communication methods at the beginning of the school year, yet many communicate through traditional forms such as quarterly parent/teacher meetings and phone calls. Because your child has special needs and communication deficits, you want more. The individualized communication plan gets you going and keeps you going, making initiation easier for both the parent and teacher. It doesn't, however, promise polished communication skills for either party—that you will gain with experience. Don't fear bungled communication— it's communication at heart, and it gives you a chance to learn. A particularly stressed parent whose house was being foreclosed sent me some creative texts about a misunderstanding, promising that karma would get me. She cooled down as I considered her stress in my response as we focused on her child's needs. From that point, every communication with the parent was kind and respectful. My favorite call from a parent came at 7:20 a.m. "Riley won't get dressed for school!" I didn't need to hear more to know that my rascally student frustrated his mother and left her with only one option— call Mrs. Oliver! Some teachers may consider the 7:20 a.m. call inappropriate, and I wondered what powers I had to make Riley get dressed, but I found the call endearing. The mother admitted her frustration later, and I never got an early call from her again.

The individualized communication plan fits any student. You may have noticed that *autism* or *ASD* are not mentioned on the forms. *All* students benefit from effective parent/teacher communication. For students with ASD, the need for communication doesn't change—parents are just more inspired to make it work. You have the added responsibility of communicating for someone who cannot always make his needs and wants known. Kudos to you for learning how to be an effective collaborator and advocate as you set the foundation for your child's kindergarten year.

The Individualized Education Program (IEP)

The thoughtful IEP best serves the child.

IDEA understands that one size doesn't fit all. IDEA was created so that your child's education wears like a tailor-made suit, rather than a mass-produced, one-size-fits-all T-shirt. It guarantees an individualized education through a legal document, the IEP. Once a child qualifies for special education, a team creates and implements the IEP annually. Parents are important members of this team.

The IEP process can be confusing and intimidating. You will learn that it consists of three consecutive steps or actions:

1. linking the child's needs to the services

2. linking the services to the providers

3. holding the providers accountable for the services.

When you understand its structure, the IEP becomes a flexible tool for building your child's education. With knowledge and a little experience, you will be an effective IEP team member.

Structure of an IEP

The IEP is built to give your child the education he needs, individualized to him. While the IEP contains many categories, special education and related services take center stage.

Special education

Once you've chosen the child's physical school, step 1 is complete. In step 2, the IEP team constructs goals specifically for your child. Regardless of the setting, either with his general education peers or in a self-contained classroom, the goals are implemented to guide your child's growth. Consider how the following goals are individualized to strengthen future progress:

- The kindergartner knows the alphabet and can read aloud with confidence. The team notes that he has no comprehension of what he is reading. The literacy goal addresses comprehension strategies.

- The kindergartner can count to 10 without error but cannot correctly count objects up to 10. A math goal focuses on teaching one-to-one correspondence as a step toward understanding the principles of more/less, addition, and subtraction.

- The kindergartner shows timidity and lack of initiative for completing classroom routines. A behavior goal teaches independence for everyday occurrences.

- The kindergartner interrupts adults and peers and doesn't share toys during play. A social goal helps the student learn to take turns during conversations and playtime.

- The kindergartner can't hold a writing utensil to print and color. The occupational therapist implements a goal to teach the tripod grip.

- The kindergartner repeats the last words of phrases said to him instead of answering questions or making relevant comments. The speech therapist's goals include tactics to expand communication skills.

IEP goals personalize the child's special education to his specific needs. Most important, only after the goals are constructed should the team determine the optimal classroom setting for your child.

Related services

The goals tell us what to do while the related services tell us how and when. The team determines the services necessary for a child to reach success, based on his individual needs. Related services appropriate for a child with ASD usually include the following:

- instruction by a special educator, sometimes referred to as an intervention specialist
- speech therapy
- occupational therapy
- physical therapy
- adaptive physical education
- counselling
- social skills group
- transportation to and from school
- music or art therapy (while these therapies have positive benefits for the child, neither is yet identified as an evidence-based practice, and the school's administration may not offer them without extensive proof of need).

Related services, with the exception of transportation, should have a corresponding goal. If the student receives speech and occupational therapies and adaptive physical education, each service provider would create a specific goal. The speech goal could focus on the comprehension of spoken language; the occupational therapy goal would work on improving cutting and writing skills; and the adaptive physical education goal would help the student learn to kick and catch a ball. The IEP states the amount of time that is dedicated to each related service, and the service provider must meet the time requirement. She can always give more, but never less.

Additional IEP sections

Most IEPs contain 12–20 pages, with goals and related services accounting for about eight of those pages. The remainder of the IEP supports knowledge of the child, justification for the IEP, and descriptions of how the IEP will be implemented. The typical IEP includes the following categories:

- *General information*—meeting date and IEP time lines; the child's and parents' data including address and phone numbers; and a blank section for other relevant information.

- *Future plans*—the team-created statement about the child's future that can include both short- and long-term plans. For example, it could state that the team would like the child to know the alphabet by the end of kindergarten and live independently as an adult. Parents, make sure your input is included in this section.

- *Child's profile*—the team's multifaceted description of your child. A good profile describes the child's likes, strengths, and needs. It gives objective evidence of the how the child has grown and where he needs support. The profile section should make reference to the following:

  - past IEPs and goals the child recently met

  - the current three-year evaluation (determines eligibility for special education)

- academic test or evaluation results
- behavior and social needs
- supporting information for related services.

- *Postsecondary transition and services*—for transition to adulthood. Don't be concerned if you see these categories on your young child's IEP. If they are included, the sections will be blank because your child is not yet approaching high school.

- *Assistive technology*—a list of assistive technology used by your child, such as modified tools for handwriting, an audio player for listening to textbooks, or a communication device.

- *Accommodations*—supports that allow the child to participate in the curriculum without changing it. Examples include access to an educational assistant, small group or individual instruction, extended time for completion of assignments, seating close to the teacher, visual aids, and keyboarding instead of handwriting.

- *Modifications*—changes made to the curriculum that modify what is being taught or tested. Examples include reduced homework and classroom assignments, use of an alternative curriculum, and grading based on IEP goals instead of the standard curriculum.

- *Least restrictive environment*—a statement confirming that a child is attending his home school or justification for an alternative school placement.

- *Testing (district and/or state)*—confirmation that the child will participate in all standardized testing, or justification if the child will be alternately assessed.

- *Meeting participants*—names and signatures of all who attended the IEP meeting.

■ *Signatures*—the parent's signature to indicate the outcome of the IEP meeting. Possibilities include acceptance of the IEP, acceptance of a change of placement, or acknowledgement of participation without accepting the current IEP or a change of placement.

Everyone finds the elements of an IEP overwhelming at first, including school team members who are new to the process. The structure of this legal document allows our knowledge of the child to fill every section of the IEP. It shouldn't be *easy*; it should be *thoughtful*.

The thoughtful IEP

You're a novice team member, and you wonder if you have a good IEP for your child. At this point, you don't have wisdom gained from years of experience to determine if the IEP will be effective. As a rule of thumb, *a thoughtful IEP is an effective IEP*. With or without experience, you can analyze your child's IEP for thoughtfulness.

The thoughtful IEP takes time and teamwork. You aren't able to see the gathering of data, the collaboration among team members, and the hours of writing that combine to create your child's IEP. You see the evidence, however, in the finished product. With your child's current IEP in hand, answer these questions:

■ Does the IEP refer to my child by name throughout the document, or is my child *the student*?

■ Does it sound like my child they're describing in the profile? Or could it be any child?

■ Do the goals capture my child's most important challenges?

■ Are the goals precise?

■ Do I understand the goals? If I were the teacher or related service provider, could I implement the goal easily?

THE INDIVIDUALIZED EDUCATION PROGRAM (IEP)

I hope you responded positively to all or most of these questions. You need to look only at the Profile and Goals for evidence of thoughtfulness.

The child's profile

First, do a visual check of the profile. It should be longer than a sentence or single paragraph. I cringed at one profile I read, "Kayla is a fifth grader at ABC Elementary School." That was it! At least it referred to Kayla by name instead of calling her *the student*.

Introduction

The profile should introduce the student and include his strengths, likes, and challenges. A profile could begin:

> Benedict is an energetic five-year-old kindergartner enrolled in general education. He enjoys Legos and trains in any form, especially Thomas the Tank Engine. Benedict likes structure and does an excellent job following class rules. He even helps other students follow the rules. Benedict enjoys tablet activities, both for learning and entertainment, but he doesn't seem as interested in the computer unless he's playing an alphabet game. Benedict has done a fine job acclimating to the classroom routines and is a cooperative student but sometimes shows anxiety. He becomes anxious when he has to leave the classroom for activities such as art, music, or lunch. During lessons, Benedict shows anxiety when he is uncertain or afraid to give the answer, even when he knows what to do. He needs encouragement to act independently.

Conversely, I've seen the child described in negative terms only:

> Because he's autistic, Benedict is stuck on rules and makes other children follow them. He won't do computer activities he is assigned and keeps switching to the alphabet game. He cries when he has to leave the classroom for lunch even though he should know the schedule by now. He knows the right answers, but refuses to show the teacher.

Which Benedict do you think will get the help he needs from the team?

Background information

The profile should give background information about the child that includes outcomes from the most recent three-year team evaluation ("Benedict's three-year team evaluation states that he would benefit from continued intervention because of his delays in the areas of social emotional skills and communication, which will adversely affect his educational performance in the areas of following directions and school rules, and attending to task completion throughout the school environment."), progress on his current IEP goals ("Benedict met his math goal with 80% accuracy, and has shown good progress in his reading goal with 75% accuracy, just five points away from the goal's 80% accuracy."), and results of any standardized tests that compare his progress to his peers ("Benedict scored 7/18 in the district's fall reading assessment, and 15/18 in the same assessment given in the spring."). It can also include information about classroom assessments ("Benedict increased the number of sight words he can read from 15 to 35 as shown in weekly classroom assessments."), and data taken for behavior and social skills ("Benedict shows enthusiasm for classroom activities, likes to be first in all of them, and pays attention if he is not upset that he has to wait his turn. Benedict averages two reactions per day when he is not first or when someone has an item he wants."). Without this information, the profile isn't individualized to your child.

The need for special education

This portion of the profile explains the child's specific areas of need as defined from the background information, especially the results of the three-year team evaluation. Benedict's evaluation indicates that he is behind his peers in language arts and math and shows deficits in speech and fine motor skills. The following examples give extracts of the profile for each area of need:

- *Speech*: Benedict has received speech services since preschool. His goals have focused on vocabulary building, social skills, and following directions. He has made wonderful progress to date in the area of communication and has met his goal to follow simple directions of one to two steps, particularly those that involve routine. Benedict continues to need work in basic concepts and expanding his sentences.

- *Occupational therapy*: Benedict receives school-based occupational therapy services to address delays in fine motor development and visual motor integration that adversely affect his performance in the classroom and throughout all school environments. Benedict can use scissors to cut within 1/4" of a straight line, and he partially cuts shapes. He cannot reproduce the letters in his name and struggles to trace letters and connect dots. Benedict can zip/button his clothing with adult assistance.

- *Language arts*: Benedict worked hard to learn all the letters of the alphabet. He met his current IEP goal for identifying letter sounds and is currently working on phonics with 30 percent accuracy for syllables, ending sounds, and rhymes.

- *Math*: Benedict met his math goal to match items, and is especially good with matching and naming shapes. He also met his math goal to count to 20 and show 1-to-1 correspondence. Benedict's next step is the concept of more/less/equal. On classroom assessments, he scores 25 percent correct with the concept of *more* and has shown no understanding of *less* and *same*.

Profiles vary. While some are organized with headings, others contain large blocks of sentences with no paragraph breaks. Regardless of its form, the profile must contain enough information to assure that the IEP is individualized. The team uses the profile to create custom learning goals for your child.

The goals

A thoughtful profile doesn't always guarantee thoughtful goals. Look for consistency between the two. If the profile discusses an area of need, the team must create a goal to address that need or explain why no goal exists to address the need. If a goal exists, the area of need must be mentioned in the profile. It sounds straightforward, but I've seen goals that seem to have dropped from the sky, with no mention of the need in the profile.

The IEP team creates effective goals because it understands the individuality of the child. We want the following properties for each goal:

- The goal is customized to the child's needs.
- The goal is understandable and precise.
- The goal should be clear enough for anyone to implement it.

Let's review some examples of goals and evaluate them with the previously mentioned criteria.

- Goal: *When Benedict is presented with two groups of objects, he will identify which group has* more, less, *or* same *with 70 percent accuracy for three consecutive weeks,* by the end of this IEP. Is the goal customized to Benedict's needs? Yes, the profile stated that he can identify *more* with 30 percent accuracy, and does not yet understand *less* or *equal*. Is the goal understandable and precise? Yes, it tells what should happen (compare two groups of objects), and gives the criteria for success (70% for three consecutive weeks). Is it clear enough for anyone to implement? We can't give a 100 percent guarantee; however, if Benedict had a substitute teacher, the sub shouldn't experience confusion in knowing how to implement this goal.

- Goal: *Benedict will leave the classroom without overreaction 100 percent of the time.* Is the goal customized to Benedict's needs? Yes. The profile mentions that Benedict's anxiety increases at times of transition. Is the goal understandable and precise? Somewhat. At first glance, we know that Benedict should leave the room without overreaction. But when should he leave the room? Anytime he wants? When the bell rings? A precise goal would indicate the parameters, such as *When Benedict transitions to lunch…* This goal does not clarify what an overreaction looks like, and the standard for meeting the goal is unrealistic. Five-year-olds who are learning how to maneuver through their world will rarely achieve 100 percent accuracy, nor do they need to. The goal's measurement is more clearly expressed as: *…he will go independently with two or fewer adult directives with 80 percent accuracy.* Is the goal clear enough for anyone to implement? No. The teacher may consider an overreaction to be running and screaming, but the sub could call hesitation an overreaction.

- Goal: *The student will participate in all lessons.* Is the goal customized to the child's needs? No. The profile didn't mention that Benedict has difficulty participating in lessons. This appears to have come from a bank of generic goals with the telltale sign of saying *the student* instead of using Benedict's name. Is the goal understandable and precise? No. The goal's lack of precision muddles the team members' ability to understand it. It does not explain what participation looks like and gives no criteria for knowing when the goal is met. Additionally, the setting for *all* lessons makes data collection unmanageable. Is it clear enough for anyone to implement? No. I can imagine the teacher ignoring this undefined goal once the frustration of taking data for every lesson proves too challenging. The substitute teacher will either scurry throughout the day to take data for all lessons, or make it up because she was too busy running the classroom. With this goal, Benedict is not receiving individualized special education.

I have rewritten some IEPs that I inherited because the goals were unmanageable, vague, or ill-suited for my students. On most, the profiles were descriptive, but the link to the goals didn't exist. Thoughtful IEP creators are like fine tailors whose suit will fit *only* the person it was designed for.

Creating the IEP

You've read about the structure of an IEP, and now you get to see how it becomes your child's unique plan. The initial IEP is created when your child qualifies for special education services. Thereafter, the IEP is reviewed and updated annually. An IEP is noncompliant as soon as it is older than 365 days. School districts have an additional incentive to keep IEPs current because they receive funding for compliant ones only.

The IEP review must occur annually, but team members can request a meeting for a review anytime throughout the year. Sometimes the team will need to amend the IEP if the student met his goals before the annual review date. Perhaps the team is meeting because the parents are concerned about academic regression or a new behavioral challenge. The team can amend the current IEP or create a new one as many times as necessary before the annual review date. Please refer to the *Checklist for Creating the IEP* in the Practical Tools section, to help keep you organized throughout the process.

Preparing for the meeting

The team sends the parent a written invitation to attend the scheduled IEP regardless of who initiated the meeting. In the meantime, all team members should be preparing for the upcoming meeting by doing the following:

- reviewing the current IEP and three-year team evaluation
- gathering data
  - standardized test results
  - recent report cards
  - IEP progress notes
  - related services progress
  - behavior and social skill observational data
- collaborating with all team members (Parents, feel free to voice your hopes and concerns).

Teams approach upcoming IEP meetings in different ways. Some teams like to come to the meeting with a blank document and supporting data and write the IEP together from scratch. Other teams complete a draft of their portion, compile everyone's input, and provide a copy to all in advance. On occasion, the parent will arrive at the meeting and see the draft for the first time. IDEA has no rules for meeting preparation. As a parent, communicate your pre-meeting needs to the other team members.

The IEP meeting

The IEP structure is predictable, and so are the majority of the meetings. At a predictable IEP meeting, you can expect the following:

- most or all team members attend
- the team reviews each section of the IEP

- team members address one another's questions and concerns
- the team makes agreed-upon adjustments to the IEP draft
- the parent agrees to implement the IEP.

The meeting may go as predicted, or it may end with unresolved issues. The team usually has an agreed-upon IEP when the day is done, but parents need to be ready for all possibilities.

Most or all team members attend

Considering busy schedules and multiple IEP meetings, some team members attend for a short while or not at all. Related service providers such as occupational and speech therapists sometimes have to juggle several meetings a day. IDEA requires that only three people be present at the IEP meeting: the special education teacher, the general education teacher, and a district representative (a principal or administrator). A parent's participation is required for three types of meetings: the initial IEP, an IEP that includes a change in placement, and the final IEP to remove the student from special education. The team is required to invite the parent to each IEP meeting, including the annual reviews. Even though a parent's participation isn't always required, your child benefits from your involvement.

The IEP meeting needs three participants, but it can have many more. Of course, we hope that each team member is able to attend the entire meeting. Parents can bring a supportive family member/ friend, an advocate, the child's outside service provider, a physician, counselor, or attorney. The school district may invite another administrator, an attorney, or psychologist. The meeting runs more smoothly when everyone knows in advance that other guests will be in attendance.

The team reviews each section of the IEP

If the meeting feels rushed and portions of the IEP are not addressed, you have the right to ask to slow down for a thorough review, or to reschedule the meeting when everyone has more time. The entire document is that important!

Remember to look for evidence of a thoughtful IEP in the Profile and Goals sections. You want to verify that the profile is complete, the goals are precise, and the two sections match the student's needs to his goals. Don't be surprised if the team doesn't understand the link between the Profile and Goals. Not everyone has been equally trained to write IEPs. If you find the Profile or Goals section lacking, you can begin the conversation by stating, "Let's give this some more thought."

Team members address one another's questions and concerns

Ask for clarification if the acronyms and terms are unclear at any time during the IEP process. Educators need to remember that the parents don't speak their jargon. Jargon resolves itself easily, as do most concerns.

High conflict, however, changes the dynamics of the meeting. This occurs when members of the team are not in agreement and cannot quickly find common ground. The discussion can be polite, anger-infused, or somewhere in between. Regardless, it's the point where the *us-against-them* mentality tends to wheedle in. The administrator won't consider the services of an educational aide; the majority of the team wants to place your child in an educational setting you don't agree with; or the parent wants a service dog in the classroom. Someone takes an immovable stance. Perhaps administration nullifies the parent's request because of budget constraints. The parents may be seeking every service and device, including unproven treatments, as an antidote to their child's autism. Or the parent and the team truly view the child's needs differently. If you find yourself in high conflict, remember FAPE (fair appropriate public education)—and remember to breathe!

The team needs to apply IDEA's *fair and appropriate* measure to the conflict. If administration denies a request for an aide because "we don't do that in this district," their position disallows consideration of your child's individual needs. If they deny it because the team believes your child will lose independence with the assistance of an aide, the discussion should continue because FAPE is being considered. Team members can experience a conflict that arises from a parent's request for a $2000 communication device for the nonverbal child. All team members acknowledge the need for enhanced communication yet further discussion is required by FAPE to determine what is appropriate for the child's current communication needs. When parents ask for specific services or devices, they narrow the team's choices. Instead they can ask for an evaluation to prove the need for further support. Data brings objectivity back into the discussion.

IDEA considered unmet parental requests and created the *Prior Notice of the Procedural Safeguards* (34 CFR 300.503)[1], often referred to as the prior written notice. The IEP team cannot end the conflict by verbally refusing parental requests for assessments or services. The team must put the following in writing:

- a description of the request that was refused

- why it was refused

- a list of alternate options considered, and why they were refused

- supporting data used to make the refusal

- other relevant factors.

---

1   idea.ed.gov.

Parents have the right to ask for mediation or due process for unresolved conflicts. Though most IEPs are accepted, parents sometimes need to rely on IDEA's procedural safeguards.

The team makes agreed-upon changes to the IEP draft

This is true in the majority of meetings as you learned above. You now have a working IEP for your child.

The parent agrees to implement the IEP

The parent signs the IEP to indicate participation, and, unless a prior written notice is in place, signs again to agree to the IEP's implementation. If you believe you have a good IEP but still have a tinge of unexplained doubt about its effectiveness, that shouldn't stop you from agreeing to its implementation. Remember that you don't have to wait another year to make changes. An IEP can be amended at any time.

As a parent and an IEP creator, I look forward to the meeting as a time to reflect aloud about the child. It's like a birthday without the cake—together we celebrate the child's personhood and growth. And we can do it more than once a year if needed!

Implementing the IEP

The IEP becomes effective on the signing date, which is usually the meeting date. It requires each service provider to carry out the goals and services as written beginning on the date it was signed. The *Checklist for Implementing the IEP*, in the Practical Tools section, will help you keep track of the steps involved in assuring the IEP is followed. Once the IEP is implemented, you will get one of three outcomes:

1. The IEP is being followed, and it works.

2. The IEP is being followed, and it needs to be adjusted.

3. The IEP isn't being followed.

Parents send their children to school and don't see the day-to-day activities that make the IEP work. IDEA knows how to prove to you that the IEP is being implemented through the progress report.

The progress report

The goal page contains a section that tells when and how the child's progress will be reported to the parent. Progress reports must be provided at least as often as report cards are issued to all children, including in the middle of each grading period if the school supplies interim reports. Progress reports should contain the following items.

- A separate report for *each* goal: each goal specifically states the growth criteria, so you should expect an individual report for each goal. Ask for individual goal reports if you receive a simple statement that "the student is showing progress."

- The method for measuring progress (assessments, observation, checklists): the goal indicates the method for measuring progress, and the progress report should refer back to this method. Methods vary; a teacher would use observation for a behavior goal, a checklist for how many times the student independently transitioned, and an assessment to determine how many addition problems the student correctly performed.

- Criteria for meeting the goal and the child's current progress (usually a percentage): it's not enough to read that your child regressed or made progress, you need the numbers ("Benedict showed no progress this reporting period, remaining at 55% accuracy.").

- A statement noting the child's progress for the period (regression, no progress, some progress, good progress, goal met): you need numbers (but not in isolation). Be certain that the report states the movement of the numbers—up for improvement and down for regression.

- Supporting notes from the service provider: they don't have to be lengthy but should personalize the report ("Benedict's percentage remained the same this period, perhaps because of the week he missed with the flu and the additional days off for inclement weather.").

The service provider creates the progress report using data gathered throughout the grading period.

The mundane mechanics of a progress report might hide the power it offers parents. If you're receiving the progress report each time report cards are issued, you have evidence that your child's IEP is being implemented. Red flags should be waving furiously if you don't receive progress reports; this indicates possible noncompliance. The IEP is a legal document that each service provider is bound to implement, and the lack of a progress report indicates the first breach—you didn't get what is required. Second, was there no progress report because the teacher or therapist took no data or ignored the goal? You don't know why, but you know to be wary.

Act immediately if you don't receive a progress report; it's your canary in the mineshaft. You want to know sooner than later that your child's IEP is being followed. The urgency of special education requires the providers and the parents to be vigilant.

IEP compliance

You receive timely progress reports, have good communication with your child's teacher, and are confident that your child is growing. This is good evidence of a compliant IEP. Conversely, you have to ask for progress reports each grading period and may or may not get them. The providers are vague when you inquire about your child's services, and you have no proof that your child is learning. These indicators point toward a noncompliant IEP. Providers cannot select which sections of the IEP they will implement and which will be glossed over.

IEP noncompliance can be in the form of neglecting to provide a related service such as speech therapy, or providing it at a level below the indicated time allotment. Sometimes a child is designated to have small group or individual instruction with a special educator but instead remains in a whole-group classroom setting. An academic goal could be ignored because the teacher said the specific skill is not in her current lesson plans for the class. Simply, an IEP is compliant when every part is implemented as written. It's still compliant when the providers do more than is written. The IEP becomes noncompliant when the providers change or delete any required actions, including goals, services, accommodations, or modifications. If the teacher tells you that your child is struggling in the classroom, being disruptive to others, or is not behaving properly, this is an opportunity for you to check on IEP compliance. After listening and acknowledging the teacher's comments, ask IEP-related questions. For instance, when the teacher says your child is disruptive in the classroom, ask if he has access to his schedule and small group instruction. Find out if he is getting accommodations that include frequent breaks. Sometimes a connection exists between your child's stress and the staff not providing IEP accommodations. It's worth investigating.

When advocating for your child to ensure a compliant IEP, talk first with the service provider. Many misunderstandings can be resolved at this level. If you reach no agreement, you can call the team together to discuss the implementation of your child's IEP. The team may realize that the noncompliant portion of the IEP is ambiguous, or that the interpretation for services differed among team members. Hopefully, all will be resolved. If not, you have recourse by filing a complaint for noncompliance. Check with your state's department of education to learn how to proceed.

Adjusting the IEP

Things change. Your child burned through his math goal and met it in three months. The goal for "hands and feet to self" is working, but he recently began to bite. The IEP that came with your child from preschool to kindergarten doesn't fit the new environment. Your child showed regression on a goal for two consecutive reporting periods. As circumstances change, the IEP can accommodate.

Any team member, parents included, can call for a review of the IEP to amend or create a new document. If a few changes need to be made, as is the case in updating a goal or clarifying a service, the amendment is an easy fix. In cases where the IEP needs an overhaul, as sometimes happens when the IEP from preschool no longer fits or when a student transfers from a different district, the team creates a new IEP that reflects current needs. Never hesitate to ask for a team meeting when you have concerns. The IEP is a flexible document that can accommodate the child's changing world.

The supportive IEP

When you unwrap the IEP, you see that it is a support, a stepping stone to your child's amazing future. Even if it seems confusing or overwhelming at times, the IEP brings unity to your child's IEP team by focusing on the most important skills he needs for continual growth.

Supporting your child's success

The strength of this legal document *supports* your child's current level of success and builds upon it. We go back to the Profile section to understand the child's present level of performance with data, assessments, and observations. It's no guessing game—the team knows precisely where the child is performing so that it can determine what he needs to get to the next level.

Supporting your child's progress

Each team member *supports* your child's progress precisely as they agreed to in the IEP. The goals were created to bridge the gap between the child's present level of performance and future gains. How exciting to see progress reports that bring the future into existence! We crafted the IEP to not only promote growth, but to also give the child the tools and support he needs to accomplish the goals.

Supporting your advocacy

The *supportive* nature of the IEP guides your advocacy. You know how to find the middle—you won't allow noncompliance, yet you won't demand that the IEP cure your child's autism. An army of advocating parents have gone before you to bring about the creation of IDEA and the IEP. They understood the need for individual support for children with disabilities. The genius of the IEP shines throughout the document as it links your child's needs to his services, the services to the provider, the provider to accountability. That will get the job done!

Academics

Your child can learn. Expect comprehensive instruction.

Academic expectations trickled down since you attended elementary school—yesterday's first grade is today's kindergarten with increased instruction and decreased playtime. Kindergartners are using technology, working independently in small groups, completing one-on-one assessments with the teacher, reading books, and writing paragraphs. Contrast this to the whole-group activities, including a nap, in your half-day kindergarten program. You may find yourself vulnerable for two reasons. First, you are inexperienced in advocating for a child with autism in elementary school; and, second, you cannot rely on your prior school experience to guide you. Knowledge sets your footing as you support your child's learning. This chapter will familiarize you with academic expectations, assessments, and interventions.

The subjects

Kindergarten entertains the 3 Rs—reading, writing, and 'rithmetic—along with science and social studies. The term "kindergarten readiness" assumes that the child has foundational knowledge that prepares him for full-day academic activities. "Readiness" is like a

Christmas wish list—you can still survive if you don't get everything you asked for. We get a clue of what basic academic skills educators hope to see in place from beginning-of-the-year assessments that are commonly given to kindergartners. The topics include the following:

- alphabet identification, upper and lower case
- number identification, zero to nine
- counting to ten or higher
- counting objects correctly
- shape identification
- color identification.

Each child develops at an individual pace socially, emotionally, and academically as any kindergarten teacher will confirm. Your child simply needs to show up for the first day of school as is. The IEP team, or the parent/teacher relationship if no IEP exists, will do the heavy lifting to craft an academic plan suitable for your child. On the last day of kindergarten, you want to be able to say, "What a difference a year makes!"

Every state uses standards that guide the academic benchmarks for public education. Because more than 40 states have adopted the Common Core standards (CCS), along with growing numbers of private schools, they will be our guide for academic subjects.

English/language arts

I have seen a wide range of language arts abilities in my kindergarten students with ASD. Some are fluent readers, some know and love the alphabet, and some find the alphabet abstract and incomprehensible. While one child can be entertained with multiple book read-alouds, the next cannot sit for even one page. The majority of my students struggle with comprehension.

From this starting point, Common Core standards (Common Core State Standards Initiative, 2015) tell us what skills we hope to see at year's end. Reading is categorized into these sub-groups:

- Foundational skills
  - print concepts
  - phonological awareness
  - phonics and word recognition
  - fluency
- Literature and informational text
  - key ideas and details
  - craft and structure
  - integration of knowledge and ideas
  - range of reading and level of text complexity
- Speaking and listening
  - comprehension and collaboration
  - presentation of knowledge and ideas
- Language
  - conventions of standard English
  - vocabulary acquisition and use.

The numerous language arts and literacy standards reflect the complexity of reading itself. As a teacher, I guide students in the skills they need to acquire for meaningful reading, but I think that reading is a neurological miracle! Let's examine how this occurs.

Foundational skills

You may remember this as phonics, starting with alphabet knowledge. We make the students aware that print follows a left-to-right, top-to-bottom, page-after-page flow, words are separated by spaces, and words we speak are represented in text. We teach the sounds of letters and blends; we rhyme and count syllables. We begin reading words by decoding (sounding them out) and by memorizing high-frequency sight words such as *I, and, they, with*. We practice fluency by reading aloud.

Literature and informational text

We're engaged in a book for storytime. Students learn to identify the characters, setting, and main event of a story. They ask and answer pertinent questions and retell the story with detail. We'll stop to identify and define unknown words. The students understand that the story has an author and an illustrator and the role that each play in creating a story. We'll even discuss genres (fiction, informational, poetry), and fit in a little time to compare and contrast characters or other stories. Students can apply the same set of skills when reading storybooks and informational texts.

Speaking and listening

Young ones with ASD will need our support for this category. Students learn to listen and take turns in conversation and in classroom social settings. They are prompted to ask questions for help, clarification, or to gain information while speaking audibly and articulately. The standards ask them to describe familiar people, places, things, and events in detail. These standards give the IEP team an excellent starting point for creating a goal for the student who needs communication support in the learning environment.

Language

By year's end, the standards aim for the students to speak in full sentences, increase the length and vocabulary used in sentences, use plurals properly, and understand how to ask a question. For writing, they will learn capitalization and ending punctuation and will write words phonologically. Students will learn the meaning of unknown words by examining the context of where the word is used. They will sort words to learn categories and will understand synonyms and antonyms.

Writing

Writing goes beyond forming alphabet letters as your child is taught to express thoughts and knowledge. I separated reading and writing because of the importance of the skill. Some educators will help a struggling reader and, in the process, delay writing because it may appear as a higher skill not reachable at this point. Not so. Writing is hard work that benefits the student by developing reflection skills, which can be taught with supports. Common Core standards for writing are the following:

- text types and purposes
- production and distribution of writing
- research to build and present knowledge.

Kindergartners can express themselves by drawing, dictating, or writing to state an opinion, inform, explain, or tell about an event. They learn to answer questions using prior knowledge or research from provided sources, and even participate in group writing activities. These standards support writing skills with knowledge of grammar, sentence structure, and spelling. My students who use three pictures to write about their day or an event from a book use the same skills of composition as their peers who draw or write words. "I ate pretzels" and "The cat ran" validly express thoughts as the student selects and orders the pictures. Regardless of the output format, the students start at the same point to use reflection skills to compose.

Math

We can count on math to be more straightforward than the sometimes abstract language arts standards. The kindergarten Common Core standards are the following:

- Counting and cardinality
  - know number names and the counting sequence
  - count to tell the number of objects
  - compare numbers
- Operations and algebraic thinking
  - understand addition as putting together and adding to, and understand subtraction as taking apart and taking from
- Numbers and operations in base ten
  - work with numbers 11–19 to gain foundations for place value
- Measurement and data
  - describe and compare measurable attributes
  - classify objects and count the number of objects in categories
- Geometry
  - identify and describe shapes
  - analyze, compare, create, and compose shapes.

Math instruction lends itself to physical and visual representations. We use everyday objects, shapes, pictures, games, and number lines to teach concepts. If a program consists only of worksheets, the student could be missing comprehension opportunities. The following examples illustrate how kindergartners can learn math with hands-on activities.

Counting and cardinality

Children with ASD may find comfort in counting—when their environment seems to be constantly changing, one through ten remains the same. However, I want my students to identify the numerals, not just memorize the order of numbers. Next, we tackle one-to-one correspondence, which shows me that the student understands numeric symbolism. The numeral three represents three objects. Students also make errors with one-to-one correspondence when they miscount. My pile of six farm animals counts out as eight on the first try—and five on the next! One object per number, please. Finally, this category teaches comparison with more/less/equal, another concept that *must* be taught with the use of manipulatives.

Operations and algebraic thinking

Counting and cardinality need to be in place before the student can move forward with operations and algebraic thinking. This category introduces simple addition and subtraction beginning with *one more* and *one less*. We use the number line not only to see the sequence of numbers as we did when learning to count, but also to move up and down the line. When the student has a grasp of more/less/equal, he is ready to apply logic to addition and subtraction. Now he is pairing two numbers, not just comparing. His understanding of more/less/equal guides the principles of *more* when you add, *less* when you subtract, and *equal* when the amount is the same. Use objects to teach addition and subtraction.

Numbers and operations in base ten

We work with the numbers 11–19 to learn the groupings of tens and ones. Some students excel in math concepts and will grasp this category with ease. Most of my students in kindergarten have struggled with this concept, especially if they have weak addition skills. I begin teaching operations in base ten by adding a rod of ten connected cubes with single cubes from one through nine to visually see how one group of ten and another group of ones defines the numbers 11–19.

Measurement and data

Students begin to understand measurement by comparing opposites: big/small, short/tall, high/low, near/far. Kindergartners don't need rulers to measure. Many curriculums include plastic cubes that snap together for children to create equal lengths with objects such as pencils and desktops. Students need correct one-to-one correspondence to count the cubes to indicate the object's length. The concept of more/less/equal comes into play when they compare which object is shorter or longer. Kindergartners learn about data through classification and counting: 13 students in the class prefer chocolate ice cream, and 11 prefer vanilla; the month of October had 12 sunny days, 15 cloudy days, and five rainy days.

Geometry

Kindergartners don't need to master the previous concepts to ace geometry. Most of my students over the years excelled with identifying and constructing shapes. First we teach the shapes and their names as one-dimensional objects. The child's environment is rich with shapes and can be used to solidify shape identification: the clock is a circle, the door is a rectangle, the sink is an oval. Next, the students learn the difference between one-dimensional and three-dimensional shapes along with accompanying vocabulary. The square becomes a cube as it goes from one to three dimensions. Students enjoy creating new shapes by combining, such as making a rectangle from two triangles. The kindergarten common core curriculum does not include standards for teaching colors. If I find a student lacking in color identification, I pair the different colored shapes as a way to reinforce colors as he learns shapes.

Science and social studies

The Common Core standards incorporate the subjects of science and social studies through informational texts. Students use reading strategies to comprehend these texts and math skills to work out scientific formulas.

Teachers extend scientific inquiry through experimentation and writing activities to document the findings. For example, after studying about healthy practices in a text, students will dot their hands with washable markers and try several ways to scrub off the "germs." They will take data on the results of washing with water only, washing a short time with water and soap, and washing with water and soap for a longer duration. Teachers hope to foster curiosity about the workings of the world in young children through scientific inquiry. Naturally occurring events serve as a springboard to teach science to young children. When the rain got louder in our classroom, we looked out the window to see hail, a less common event than rain or snow in our area. I stopped our lesson so that we could watch the bouncing ice on the street for its short duration. I prepared a science lesson about hail, in accordance with the common core standards, and presented it the next day while the memory was fresh. Science lessons engage the students when their everyday world is drawn into them.

Social studies at the kindergarten level instructs students about government and society through everyday occurrences. Society has rules; the classroom has rules. We live in a larger community (city, country) with many subsets: neighborhood, school, family. Informational texts support the child's understanding of and responsibilities regarding being part of a culture, and the teacher uses classroom occurrences as learning opportunities. When I teach my students the art of sharing and turn taking, it supports the students' social skills and fulfills a social studies lesson simultaneously. We can reinforce social studies in the books we read during storytime and in literacy lessons. The bear cubs live in a community with a family and neighbors; the curious monkey needs to learn rules to behave in public; and Goldilocks should respect the property of others! Social studies lessons abound in life and in literature.

Assessments

Within the first month of kindergarten, your child probably will be assessed for kindergarten readiness skills. Some assessments cover pre-reading and pre-math skills, while others add the domains of science, social studies, social/emotional skills, motor skills, and communication. The assessment has multiple purposes, none of which determines if your child will remain in kindergarten. Parents and teachers want to know how to plan suitable learning opportunities; administrators need to know how to make the kindergarten program effective; and state policymakers use the information to document population trends and future needs.

You can access a free kindergarten readiness test online if you are curious about your child's profile. The website *KinderIQ* provides a basic evaluation with 45 quick questions from five domains. If you choose to enter your child's birth date (no name necessary), the results will rank your child's score with those his same age. Once on the website *(KinderIQ.com)*, click "Kindergarten Readiness Test" from the selection bar at the top of the page. Click "Go" to begin the assessment.

The No Child Left Behind Act ushered in a climate of continual assessments that begin in kindergarten and cease only upon high school graduation. Your child will be given pre- and post-assessments to measure yearly academic growth, yet these assessments can occur more often than at the start and end of each year. The trend is to administer the assessments on computers, which can be challenging for new kindergartners. I've watched these young students in September sit at the computer, ignoring the mouse, swiping the screen with their fingers, hoping for some action! The results of these assessments are used to categorize the students (intensive needs, on target, or advanced) and plan instruction accordingly.

You may receive a report about a high-stakes academic assessment that indicates your child's annual growth. Unless the results affect your child's classroom placement, which they rarely do, you can accept them with healthy skepticism. Consider the variables at play in these assessments. What accommodations/modifications were provided, if any? Did your child have a good night's sleep prior to taking the test? How long did your child have to take the test, and was he given any breaks? Were test questions related to instruction your child received that year? Was the test given at the end of the year to determine a year's growth, or was it given in March, or even December? Students progress at uneven, individual rates. A snapshot assessment gives us the picture for that day only and is not a full measure of a child's growth over time.

These assessments measure growth and guide instruction, but they do not determine grades on the report card. The teacher uses weekly assignments, observation, and tests to compile a grade that represents your child's progress. Kindergarten grades appear as letters to indicate a level of performance, such as P for proficient, S for satisfactory, and N for needs improvement. The grading scale of A through F that is based on the percentage of correct answers is usually reserved for higher grades.

If your child has an IEP, you should expect to receive a progress report each time report cards are issued. The progress report lets you know how your child is responding to his goals. If a goal is met before the IEP's annual review is due, the IEP should be amended to nullify the goal and add another with the team's agreement. Finally, be certain to request progress reports if they do not accompany your child's report card. It is your assurance that the IEP is being followed.

Interventions

The kindergartner with ASD will be able to access the curriculum through accommodations (adaptations that do not change content) and modifications (a change to the content). Interventions can range from simple to complex, but the purpose remains consistent: the intervention must match the student's learning needs. Interestingly, accommodations made for those with special needs cross over and help others in the population. Changes made for students with ASD can help students who have sensory sensitivities, have AD/HD, or learn more effectively with visual representations.

The work area

An organized, uncluttered work area can support a ready mind for learning. In general, all materials not in use should be out of sight, preferably behind doors or neatly stacked on shelves. Walls should contain only the information that promotes the student's understanding of his day (e.g. schedule, class rules) and be free from posters and papers. Lesson materials should be presented as needed. For a more thorough understanding of an optimal teaching environment, I recommend the book *Setting up Classroom Spaces that Support Students with Autism Spectrum Disorders* (Kabot and Reeve, 2010). Accept that the classroom's physical environment is dictated by the teacher; however, as a team member, you can make suggestions if you believe the environment can be more supportive to your child's needs.

English/language arts and writing

Children with ASD present with communication and socialization challenges, which affect language arts abilities. Kindergartners are expected to express their learning verbally as they participate in groups, so how do we accommodate the echolalic or nonverbal child who needs prompting to be part of a group? The following suggestions are guidelines for adjusting the learning to fit the child's needs:

- Support verbal instruction with pictures and objects.

- Use first/then or first/next/last visual prompts to support organization.

- Teach the child with ASD individually and in small groups.

- Allow the child to have hands-on use of pictures and objects to support learning (physical alphabet letters instead of a letter line).

- Have the student demonstrate knowledge by pointing to pictures or objects.

- Simplify or reduce the number of demands in a task.

- Modify literature by retyping it with picture/symbol writing software or by highlighting key words in text.

- Create sentences that leave the last word blank with picture choices as a way to help a child begin to express himself in writing.

Teachers select accommodations and modifications that work both for them and the student, and you will see variety from class to class.

Math

We think of math as a concrete, not abstract, subject. Consider, though, that a squiggle on a piece of paper represents the number three, which means three items of any variety. Now it doesn't look as concrete. Kindergarten mathematics *must* include the use of objects (manipulatives) to teach counting, operations, measurement, and geometry. Allow the student to learn first through objects and then begin to transfer the knowledge to paper. For example, the student learns that seven is greater than four when comparing two sets of train cars. The student can transfer the information into a number sentence on paper: $7 > 4$. Once the child fully comprehends the concept, the objects won't be necessary.

Use the child's interests to support lessons. You help your child's teacher teach by informing her of your child's interests that change over time. My student who loved amusement parks (who used to love trains) did not comprehend "one less" until I drew a roller coaster on paper and made cut-out cars. He selected from sentence strips that explained why a car had to leave—needed new wheels, left to get washed, had a broken seatbelt—and would physically remove a car and count the remaining pieces.

Sometimes students with ASD are impatient with repeating lessons for skills they have mastered. The teacher needs to reduce frustration by moving forward with new challenges once the student has demonstrated knowledge. The flip side of this coin is the student who perseverates on what he already knows. I have a student who stops math lessons to count to 100. I use these perseverations as rewards for a job well done: first name the shapes, and then count to 100!

Science and social studies

Science and social studies are supported through literacy and math skills. Many curriculums have monthly themes that encompass fictional and informational texts to teach comprehension of stories, emotions, community structures, and science principles. For example, my social studies themes included rules for September, and family and community celebrations for December. Science themes focused on weather for January, and things that grow for May. The interventions used for literacy and math can also be incorporated into the subjects of science and social studies.

Influence of cognitive theories

Chapter 5 discusses the cognitive framework that is present in varying degrees for those with ASD. I see the effects daily as I deliver academic instruction. Some children have difficulty with short-term memory, so I need to provide visual supports and give them prompts to help them stay on task. Others can be impulsive and disorganized and benefit from clear expectations and pictures that show the steps necessary to complete an assignment. Sometimes a student with ASD loses sight of the crux of the lesson because he shifts the focus to a preferred interest, and then has difficulty refocusing his attention back to the lesson.

Your ability as an advocate will increase as you help teachers understand how the cognitive theories affect your child. When the teacher's understanding is clarified, she will be able to construct effective lessons that support your child's learning needs. Chapter 5 provides examples of how executive function, theory of mind, and central coherence influence your child's learning experiences.

Learn a mile in your child's shoes

Now that you're aware of kindergarten's rigorous academic standards, you understand why your child might come home exhausted from a long day at school. Just like his typical peers, he put effort into learning without the luxury of a nap. Unlike his peers, he worked extra hard to communicate, socialize, and adjust to his environment. This is a super-sized workload for a five-year-old!

Terminology

Teachers use abundant education-specific vocabulary and acronyms. If an unfamiliar term makes its way into a parent/teacher discussion, you can ask for clarification and refer to the following list. You may want to bookmark this page for future reference.

- *Accommodation*: included in the IEP. The alteration of how a lesson, assignment, or test is presented that gives the student access to the curriculum without changing its purpose and content. For example, we can accommodate a student by giving him more time to complete an assignment, allowing the use of graphic organizers and visuals, letting him keyboard instead of write by hand, or presenting instruction in a small group.

- *Assessment*: can be used interchangeably with "test," however, the function of an assessment is to measure what a child knows at a specific point. *Assessments* give us scores that influence how to teach, where *tests* influence grades. See *Pre- and Post-Assessments*.

- *Benchmark*: from the IEP. The goal is meted out into time segments that plan how a child will learn a skill. For example, the goal of learning the letters of the alphabet could have several benchmarks: (1) Child will identify eight letters by October 15; (2) Child will identify 16 letters by December 15; (3) Child will identify all letters by February 15.

- *Common Core State Standards (CCSS)*: an American education initiative that lists what students are expected to know by the end of each grade, kindergarten through 12th, in English/language arts/literacy and math. The majority of states adopted the CCSS in 2010, and, as the controversy over the standards continues, some states are rescinding the adoption for their own standards.

- *Extended standard*: CCSS that parse each skill in order to design reachable expectations for students with disabilities. Extended standards are created by individual states, and not all states who have adopted CCSS offer this adaptation.

- *Goal*: from the IEP. After the team creates a profile of the child's strengths, needs, and current performance levels, goals are created that are unique to the child's needs. Each goal is implemented through benchmarks or objectives.

- *Grades*: the indication of performance for a single assignment or for a measured period of time. Some kindergarten programs grade with the traditional A, B, C, D, or F. Others use letters as indicators of levels (S for satisfactory, N for needs improvement).

- *High-stakes testing*: tests whose function is to influence important decisions (Does a student graduate?) and accountability (Are schools and teachers effective?). Results can influence school funding and policies.

- *IDEA*: Individuals with Disabilities Education Act. Federal law that ensures special education services are provided at no cost to eligible students in public schools.

- *IEP*: a product of IDEA, the Individualized Education Plan. This legal document describes how the school will support the child's unique needs for special education.

- *Manipulatives*: physical objects that are used to teach concepts, especially in math.

- *Modification*: included in the IEP. Changes to a lesson, assignment, or test that affect what is being measured in the curriculum. For example, a student's homework questions are reduced by half, a student uses a simplified text, or grading is based on IEP goals and not on curriculum-related tests.

- *NCLB*: 2001 educational law, No Child Left Behind. Based on belief that standards-based education with measureable goals and regular assessments will improve student outcomes. Requires each state to develop assessments in literacy, writing, and math.

- *Objective*: from the IEP. A goal is divided into smaller portions that plan how a child will learn a skill. For example, the goal to increase comprehension may have these supporting objectives: 1) Child will answer "who" and "what" questions; 2) Child will identify the main character; 3) Using pictures, child will sequence the events of the story.

- *Pre- and Post-assessments*: used to determine what a child knows and how instruction will be adjusted accordingly. A pre-assessment measures what a child knows about a concept before it is taught. The results guide the teacher's instruction and help determine if more background knowledge is necessary for student comprehension. A post-assessment checks the effectiveness of student learning and reveals if reteaching is necessary.

- *Progress report*: from the IEP. The tool to monitor progress for annual goals. The written report should indicate each goal and whether (or how much) progress was made. Parents should receive progress reports at regular intervals as indicated on the IEP, usually each time report cards are issued.

- *Report card*: the formal report provided to parents at the end of each grading period with grades (or indicators of levels) for all subjects and indicators for classroom behaviors.

- *Test*: a measure of knowledge that is used to determine grades. Differs from assessments that are used to guide instruction.

Cognitive Theories

Support and patience win the race.

You want to understand your child. Early childhood development resources abound, as do books, blogs, and websites about ASD. Have you ever wished you could find the two subjects combined into one resource? That someone could explain to you why *this* behavior is age-appropriate, and *that* behavior is influenced by ASD? Parenting can seem like guesswork; and those with a first-born with ASD are further challenged because they have no background in observing a typically developing child. We need knowledge that will help us guide our children to adulthood.

Since your child's diagnosis, you have entered the complex arena of ASD, beginning with the *Diagnostic and Statistical Manual of Mental Disorders of the American Psychiatric Association* (APA, 2013). Most likely, this was your introduction to new vocabulary such as perseveration, echolalia, and reciprocity. You go on an information hunt through formal research, junk science, personal accounts, and opposing opinions. In your search, you come across executive function, theory of mind, and central coherence, and wonder how these theories pertain to your child.

No resource or theory can tell you all you need to know. On a practical level, however, the cognitive theories give you a framework of understanding that leads to interventions, support, and insight into future development. Complex theories can be parsed and repackaged to contain practical tools that will help your child gain skills and independence.

Executive function

Executive function is our brain's traffic controller that supports how we make our way through each day. It resides in the neocortex, the front and newest section of the human brain. You may see it referred to as "executive dysfunction" to describe maladaptive traits not only for those with ASD, but also with attention deficit or other disorders. Of the three theories, I find the majority of my kindergarten interventions are geared toward executive function challenges. We have communication supports in place that become second nature, and we're always looking for opportunities to enhance social connections. Yet when I review what I need to do to achieve cooperation and participation, the majority of the interventions are related to executive function: initiating and paying attention. As my former students mature, I note that they continue to benefit from interventions for executive function weaknesses. I understand why Hala, Rasmussen and Henderson (2005) and his fellow researchers believe that executive dysfunction may be the central deficit that is at the root of other observed impairments in ASD.

What it's good for

Executive function helps self-regulation. Moraine (2012, p.15) defines it by saying: "we use our executive functions to express how we *think*, what we *feel*, and what we *do* in relation to the world around us." Consider the skills supported by executive functions:

- *Attention*—focusing to understand what you need to do or learn or to execute plans.
- *Working memory*—keeping current information in mind to initiate and complete a task.

- *Organization*—preparing in advance for the successful completion of a task or activity; keeping order with routines.

- *Planning*—ordering the steps of a task from beginning to completion.

- *Time management*—planning and acting to accomplish chores, activities, and goals at the opportune time to avoid delay or consequence.

- *Inhibition*—refraining from an initial thought/action until judging its appropriateness.

- *Motivation*—having the internal or external pressure to act.

- *Initiative*—beginning the thoughts and actions required to move forward on a task or goal.

- *Cognitive flexibility*—exhibiting the capability to accept change and reroute plans or actions.

What the challenges look like

As you review the list, select and prioritize three categories where you believe your child needs the most support. We can overwhelm ourselves and our child when we try to fix all things at the same time. You will find that your child, if he follows the pattern of most, will need support in the top three categories throughout his educational career. Remember, too, that learning a successful intervention for an area is going to look different according to the circumstances and people involved. If your child learns to transition by getting ready for school and leaving the house, he will need an entirely different lesson to change activities when playing with peers.

You needn't worry about ineffectiveness if you don't address all executive function traits. They are interrelated, so if you select your top three, you will be supporting many skills. Challenges in executive function for kindergartners can look like the following.

Attention

Your child:

- can't sit in a chair for the lesson
- needs multiple redirections for simple tasks
- goes to the wrong area in the classroom for the current task
- misses guidance/instructions
- doesn't respond when you or the teacher attempt to gain his attention.

Working memory

Your child:

- can't execute a two-step task ("throw your trash away and line up")
- shows difficulty remembering the steps of a task (e.g. when his coat goes on before his backpack)
- bumbles a routine he usually gets right
- can't recall a character's name in a story just read to him
- forgets how many items he counted and begins again.

Organization

Your Child:

- can't complete simple tasks independently
- begins a task in the middle (cuts before he colors)
- jumbles his work area items (crayons on the floor, papers scattered)
- doesn't clean up after himself
- loses things often.

Planning

Your child:

- can't sequence events to tell you about something that has happened
- doesn't know how to use free time if not allowed to perseverate on his favored activity
- starts, but rarely finishes, a project he showed interest in (drawing a picture, making a cardboard-box robot)
- wants to play a video game but doesn't gather all the necessary system parts
- runs outside to play with improper clothing.

Time management (at this age, adults take charge of the majority of the child's time)

Your child:

- doesn't show comprehension of time (yesterday/today/tomorrow)
- can't judge how long an activity will take
- lacks opportunities to complete a task independently within a timeframe
- doesn't comprehend consequences for missed deadlines
- doesn't have the negotiation skills to extend a deadline.

Inhibition

Without inhibition, your child, for example:

- runs away from a lesson in progress
- stops participation to pursue his favored activity
- interrupts, or answers questions in a group without waiting to be called upon

- throws materials when he's frustrated

- grabs toys from other children without asking first.

Motivation
Your child:

- perseverates on his favored activity only

- sits and does nothing with excessive patience when given a work demand

- responds inconsistently to preferred reinforcements as motivation for completing a task

- seems stubborn

- tantrums when an adult tries to promote participation.

Initiative
Your child:

- acts confused when directed to begin a task

- depends on adults to begin his project

- excels at procrastination

- looks lazy

- experiences difficulty with transitioning or switching tasks.

Cognitive flexibility
Your child:

- as with initiative, finds transitions and task switching difficult

- can't apply knowledge across settings ("keep your hands to self in classroom *and* cafeteria")

- shows frustration or shuts down when he has to change his direction of thought during a lesson

- resists unlearning wrong information to replace it with correct information (the alphabet ends in *x, y, z,* not *x, y, n* [for "and"], *z* as it sounds in the song)

- can't quickly monitor and change behavior (continues to "scream-talk" after he gains the object of his desire).

Supporting executive function

Give your child with executive function challenges the most effective support—understanding. Peace reigns when the adult understands that the child isn't lazy, stubborn, or rebellious but instead has cognitive difficulties. The child who is perceived as lazy experiences demands for compliance and punishments; the same child who is perceived to have executive dysfunction is offered interventions and motivators.

Theory of mind

Theory of mind (ToM) gives humans the ability to play social chess (Baron-Cohen, 1997). We can predict what others are thinking and judge how our words and actions will affect them *before* we act. ToM allows us to view ourselves and others as separate entities while, at the same time, helping us make the human connection. ToM isn't something we think about as we use it daily; it's simply there for us, like our eyesight and hearing. You take notice only when it goes missing or is impaired. Those affected with ToM challenges could have been wired that way since birth, or the challenges may have resulted from a severe brain injury or stroke. You can imagine how your daily life would be changed if you had a sight or hearing impairment. Anyone who has difficulty inferring others' mental states is dealing with a handicap, too.

What it's good for

ToM sets the foundation for friendships, partnering, successful school and work careers, effective communication, and, most important, making the human connection. Consider how these relationships are supported by the attributes of ToM.

Social understanding

We make hundreds of snap decisions on a typical day, most with ease and agility, in response to our social experiences. The ever-flowing social world requires that the players use their innate abilities for every interaction. Baron-Cohen (1997) studied how those with ASD may experience *mindblindness*, the absence of that inborn ability to engage in the social environment. They are left in the dust of social interactions because they haven't formed the ability to mind read as most humans do with ease and without training. My kindergartners miss opportunities to play with their typical peers at recess because of a lack of social understanding. A boy will run up to one of my students, look at him excitedly, tag him on the shoulder, and run away. Instead of engaging in a game of chase, my student remains standing in the same spot, unaware that he was just invited to play.

Behavioral prediction

No one formally teaches us how to predict others' behavior. Experience can improve our prediction skills but, nonetheless, the ability comes pre-packaged. Without giving it a second thought, we use our prediction skills to survive the day. We offer deference to our boss and tease with our coworker, not vice versa. Imagine the turmoil we'd be in if our day went awry because of faulty—or no—predictions. A young girl in my class lived for the days we had bubbles at recess. When she was left empty-handed after the bubbles were distributed, she simply grabbed a bottle out of the hand of another child. She was innocently clueless that her actions would make her peers angry.

Social interaction

In a social context, the *hidden curriculum* refers to unwritten social rules that people instinctively know. This, coupled with prediction, creates meaningful social interactions. Myles, Trautman and Schelvan (2004) explain that the lack of hidden curriculum knowledge results in a social-cognitive learning disability. While the typical person can maneuver through the social world, those with ASD have persistent problems cracking the codes that support interactions. I watched an outgoing older student with ASD in our elementary school try to engage his peers. He interrupted conversations and activities to talk about computer programming and, more often than not, his peers walked away from him. He didn't know how to engage, share topics, follow the conversation, or determine if he talked too much. He needed specific instruction to learn what his peers know instinctively.

Communication

Communication links us together as humans; lack of communication creates aloneness. Some traits of ASD, such as mindblindness, threaten to isolate those on the spectrum. When we encourage the human connection, we support positive mental health and its benefits for our loved one with ASD.

What the challenges look like

Research by Sinha and colleagues (2014) posits that impaired "predictability" is at the core of autism. The barrage of surprises when your child cannot predict outcomes can result in a manifestation of traits such as repetitive behaviors, social and language deficits, and sensory issues. This hypothesis regarding the central importance of "predictability" is undergoing testing with a focus on what impairs prediction in the brain.

Meanwhile, ToM relies heavily on prediction, and the lack of that ability in the kindergartner with ASD can be seen in the following examples.

Can't identify simple emotions

Your child:

- may identify happy and mad as his emotions, but lacks the self-knowledge of most: cannot identify anxious, nervous, frightened, worried, sad, excited, embarrassed, proud, uncomfortable

- doesn't engage with peers because their range of emotions can be confusing, overwhelming

- doesn't respond to others' emotions typically (laughs at the expression of anger)

- can't identify the simple emotions of a character in a book, thus impeding comprehension

- doesn't know that he is boring the listener with exhaustive information on his favorite topic.

Can't pretend

Your child:

- insists on the literal (it's a box, *not* a castle)

- ignores toys, or uses toys as objects and not as tools to create playful situations

- negates playtime with peers because he can't engage in pretend play

- can't comprehend a storybook that incorporates pretending

- doesn't understand age-appropriate figurative language, metaphors, sarcasm.

Can't determine another's perspective

Your child:

- believes that you are experiencing the world identically to him (my student got angry with me because I didn't know where he put his toy; if we had the same mind, I should have remembered)

- doesn't realize that his interests are not yours, or that you have interests different from his

- doesn't take part in reciprocal play if the activity is not his choice

- doesn't understand that his actions caused a change in the peer's emotions (took a toy away, made peer angry)

- loses interest in literature if challenged to see the character's perspective (if the story's character wants ice cream, the student will either want his own flavor or be uninterested because ice cream is not important to him).

Expresses empathy differently

Your child:

- can't respond with typical empathy when he is unable to identify others' emotions

- seems emotionally absent when observing a friend who is sad or worried

- sometimes shows empathy for pets or animals, but not to those close to him

- may not comprehend why the "hands to self" rule is important because he does not realize that hitting hurts others

- rarely offers to help when he sees an obvious need, such as opening the door when your hands are full.

Supporting theory of mind

Children mature, and the child with ToM challenges also will grow in his ability to pretend, understand others' perspectives, identify emotions, and demonstrate empathy. Our students need abundant exposure, instruction, and practice to experience what most take for granted.

Have you heard that people with ASD don't have empathy? Myth! ToM weaknesses make the expression of empathy more challenging, but we can't know what's in the mind and heart of a person with ASD, especially when he has difficulty expressing it. I've watched young children with ASD show empathy: a young boy cries for a limping dog he sees at recess; a kindergartner asks for a Band-Aid for the classroom assistant's hangnail; peers hug a classmate after I explained that his mother died. Believe that empathy is there. Give children with ASD more time and instruction to find its expression.

Carol Gray describes the use of social stories (2010) to teach emotions, behaviors, and routines. These narratives objectively instruct about varied topics such as getting dressed, allowing proper personal space, going to birthday parties, and refraining from hitting others. Social narratives, especially those made specifically for the child, teach ToM skills. It's all about supporting the human connection.

Central coherence

Central coherence allows you to see the forest from the trees. It gives you the ability to identify all parts of a situation, and then comprehend how they coalesce into a big picture (Collucci, 2011). It answers the question, "What's the main point?" and creates an understanding of the whole at the expense of the details. For example, a college professor told our class that she wanted us to leave with big ideas. She wasn't concerned if we forgot some details because she knew that we would be inspired and reformed by the big ideas. She was a *see the forest from the trees* professor. The chemistry lecturer who insists that you retain every vocabulary term and theory is a *trees* professor. We would be overwhelmed if, for every situation, we needed to keep all details in mind. Working memory can't hold that much information! Instead, we summarize so that we can work with the big ideas and retrieve the details as needed.

What it's good for

Central coherence helps you find the core purpose so that you can prioritize your thoughts and behavior accordingly. When you're in a long line at the return counter, you use central coherence to concisely state the problem without going into a lengthy explanation. You use central coherence after you've had an argument with your spouse—the big picture is that you both love each other and you're committed; you're not going to divorce over how to clean the kitchen. Central coherence is at play when you read a book, too. You gather all the details to form an overall understanding of the author's intent.

Weak central coherence, or should I say detail-ability, can be a strength. Instead of having weak global processing, Happé and Firth (2006) say you can have superior local processing. Perhaps Thomas Edison used superior local processing to invent a working light bulb! Many careers require a focus on details: engineering, computer technology, accounting, medicine, science, and research.

What the challenges look like

Sometimes the person with weak central coherence walks in circles among the trees and can't find his way out of the forest. Many forests, in fact: the forest of resentment, the forest of distractibility, the forest of rule enforcement. Interventions act as the guide out of the trees.

Conversation

Many with ASD are verbal, but their pragmatic use of language is limited (Collucci, 2011). Weak central coherence can cause tunnel vision that sabotages effective communication. When the speaker spotlights his own thoughts and ideas to the detriment of understanding the main point of the conversation, weak central coherence in your child can be characterized as follows:

- he offers a fountain of details to answer a simple question

- he switches the topic abruptly to talk about his interests

- he makes the listener feel like a cog—the speaker just needs someone/anyone to hear him

- he doesn't show interest in the listener's ideas and viewpoints

- he doesn't use reciprocity: he turns the conversation into his monologue.

Distractibility

Collucci (2011) notes that the person who experiences weak central coherence can be overwhelmed by what would be minor details to others. You may see distractibility expressed in your child's behavior similar to the following examples:

- he tantrums because a puzzle piece is missing, the cereal box is not on the *right* shelf, or the teacher gave him the *wrong* colored box of crayons

- he reads only one favored page of a book without enjoying the entire story

- he adheres to a walking route where he goes out of his way to touch environmental items of interest

- he won't eat if food is not presented as he wants (different foods can't touch)

- he overreacts to a minor correction (cries when you redirect him to line up).

Memory

Memory for detail is a two-sided coin. Those with a focus on detail have ready-to-use knowledge at their fingertips. They also remember, and can be tortured by, the details of stressful situations. Without understanding the big picture that everyone makes mistakes and can be forgiven, their relationships require more work and patience. Consider the following examples:

- brings up injustices days, weeks, years, after they occurred with the same emotion as if it happened today

- holds a grudge or shows resentment about past injustices (Collucci, 2011)

- repeatedly needs to resolve the same emotional trauma

- acts like a scorekeeper to remind others how many times they wronged him.

Rules

Rules *rule* for the person who needs structure to know how to maneuver the social world. Collucci (2011) explains that those who have difficulty focusing on the whole instead of the parts can tend to be strict rule followers and enforcers. You may recognize some responses of young children who are rule followers:

- he spends recess time informing the adults of children who break playground rules

- he lacks flexibility when children change rules in a game: he may quit playing

- he scolds classmates when they chat while the teacher is out

- he tells strangers to stop smoking because that is a rule for good health

- he becomes anxious when you drive through a yellow light.

Supporting central coherence ▪▪▪▪▪▪▪▪▪▪

Children need a roadmap that delineates the trees from the forest. They need specific instruction and practice to gain skills that support weak central coherence. A speech therapist does much more than teach the formation of sounds—she teaches the pragmatic use of language. Some young students don't receive speech therapy if they are verbal; however, their need for pragmatic instruction shouldn't be ignored. Parents often supplement school-based speech therapy with private speech therapy, which can include a social skills group that gives children the opportunity to practice new skills together. Finally, cognitive behavior therapy offers help for many who experience weak central coherence challenges.

Building on your knowledge ▪▪▪▪▪▪▪▪▪▪

Because you've read this primer about the cognitive theories, you've bolstered your ability to understand your child and his actions. You won't shy away the next time you hear executive function, theory of mind, or central coherence; you'll be able to build on your knowledge. You even may seek further resources about the theories.

More good news—your child's strengths at age five will be his strengths throughout his lifetime. The interventions you implement now for your young child's challenges will promote skills and independence as he continues to mature. Because you taught your disorganized kindergartner an intervention to put away his toys, with help, your child can take skills from that task and apply them to organizing homework in middle school, completing projects in high school, and showing up on time for work as an adult.

You will become more confident as an advocate as you explain the theories' principles to teachers. *Executive function*: your child isn't lazy; he has challenges that can shut him down if he doesn't have support. *Theory of mind*: your child *does* have empathy, but it may be expressed differently. *Central coherence*: attention to details can be a strength.

One of the first things you noticed as a parent of a child with ASD is that there are those who get it, and those who don't. Some relatives and friends offer you empathy while others don't understand why you can't erase ASD with stronger discipline. In your child's educational career, you will encounter some teachers and school personnel who don't always get it. You will become an educator to the educators as you advocate for your child. In time, as knowledge and understanding increase about ASD, perhaps the representative puzzle piece can be replaced with the idea light bulb. We can figure out this puzzle!

Communication and ASD

Communication creates the human connection.

You are one of the experts who will help your child with social communication, a core challenge for those with ASD. Your child will receive the invaluable services of many speech-language therapists as he grows toward adulthood, but you will be his consistent supporter. Let's bring to the forefront the skills you, the expert, have been using all along to support your child.

Connecting through conversation

Before you understood ASD, could you imagine yourself carrying on a conversation with a person who is mute? Or listening to a monologue about a child's favored topic and not being able to add input? Or having the last three words of every sentence you spoke repeated back to you? Your world has expanded quite a bit; and because you understand, the world of your child has expanded, too.

We need to engage in meaningful conversations with children who have ASD. This may seem obvious, but all too often I have forgotten to verbalize my thoughts with children on the spectrum and have observed the same from others. The communication and social deficits of ASD create barriers to the natural flow of conversation. Add to this a tendency to focus intensely on narrow interests, and children on the spectrum experience yet another hindrance to shared communication. A sad formula for loneliness could be in place unless children with ASD are actively engaged in meaningful human interactions.

Conversations are social, collaborative events where new understandings can emerge because of the interaction. They occur throughout each day for many purposes—to share information, clarify, make plans, complain, or compliment. Regardless of the purpose, each conversation has the goal of connection. Conversations are two-sided; we are confident that we can offer the connection by initiating conversation, and we are hopeful that the connection can be made and maintained even if we don't see immediate evidence. Many children on the spectrum struggle as they make efforts to connect through conversation. If frustration mounts and successful interaction is rare, the child with ASD may give up.

Resisting aloneness

Consider the challenge for anyone with ASD to create and maintain the human connection. I recall poignant insights that formed my understanding of ASD, communication, and making the human connection. Exkorn (2005) said that aloneness may not be a preference, and that scientific studies show that parts of the social brain of people with ASD may be weak as a result of lifelong social deprivation. Tantam (2009) analogizes the *interbrain* of individuals on the spectrum to stand-alone computers, as opposed to the *interbrain* of the neurotypical population, which is connected by the Internet. He surmises that those with ASD sense the aloneness and are aware of being different and cut off. How unfortunate it is when the child with ASD is avoided because of the misinformed belief that he prefers aloneness; when the nonverbal child with ASD doesn't have anyone initiate a conversation or discuss a relevant topic because a one-sided conversation feels unnatural; or when an initiated conversation by a child with ASD is cut short because his classmate is taken aback by the social awkwardness.

Children on the spectrum are not void of relating; in fact their perspective often includes warmth and enthusiasm. One of my students who loves cats presses his head close to me as cats do to show affection; another initiates a game of chase with his nonverbal classmate and both share uproarious laughter. Children on the spectrum deserve the human connection, deficits or not.

Conversers need to take a leap of faith when connecting to a child with ASD. The interaction can be missing reliable intuitive feedback such as eye contact, shared attention, and body-language confirmations. In some instances conversations will be carried on completely by you; in others the child with ASD will dominate the conversation or spin out on tangents. Those who converse with children on the spectrum will not always receive instantaneous reinforcers typically present in everyday conversations. Nonetheless, the child with ASD needs the connection that occurs when humans join to create meaning in conversation.

Being an interpreter and converser: Communication starts at home

Tanguay (2001, p.38) explains that a child with nonverbal disabilities will tend to show preference to one parent as "the person who interprets the mystifying world around them, and the culture that the child doesn't understand." Her insight christened me with the title of *interpreter* and helped me realize a core need of children with ASD. I've learned to interpret the child's social world through modeling and conversations, even with those who have limited verbal ability. Tantam (2009) proposes that only the good communicators, like a strong Internet connection, might actually succeed in connecting with the impaired *interbrain* of those on the spectrum. It follows that our next title is *good communicator* or more simply, *converser*.

Children on the spectrum should not be excluded from meaningful conversations and human connections because of their social and communicative impairments and limited verbal ability. The blind have their cane and brail; the deaf have sign language; and children with ASD should have their interpreter and converser.

Creating opportunities to connect

Conversations are natural human events that can fit in anywhere, anytime. Because of their casual nature, the use of conversations to expand the world of children with ASD is an easy intervention that doesn't feel like intense therapy work. Here are some ideas to incorporate as you take on the interpreter and converser roles.

Remember to talk!

We tend to mirror one another in human actions, so if your child is silent, you may be silent also or limit verbalizations to directives only. You might feel awkward at first as you begin to converse, and that's okay. It becomes more natural as you continue to engage.

Use pronouns and full sentences

Even though your child may exhibit language delays, you needn't simplify your conversational style. Instead of saying, "Simon see bird?" be more natural and descriptive. "Look in that tree, Simon. I see a red cardinal!" Children with ASD can have difficulty with pronouns, confusing them or not using them. Be your child's model when you say, "I like your picture, Simon! You're a good artist" instead of "Mommy like Simon's picture!"

Be authentic

Keep the conversation on subjects you would normally talk about. The conversation doesn't have to be formal or preplanned but instead can spring from the day's events and concerns. You can use conversations to discuss emotions and reactions to the day's happenings and, hopefully, to co-create a better understanding of life. You can be sure some conversations will center on your child's authentic, perseverative topic; this is your chance as interpreter to try some turn taking and expansion of subject matter.

Take advantage of multiple opportunities

Don't be concerned that your child isn't listening, or that the topic is over his head. A speech therapist recommended that a young boy's parents talk to him all the time and use an extensive vocabulary. The parents relayed that they ran into this same speech therapist when the boy was in grade school, and recalled her directive to talk all the time, telling her it took a lot of effort on their part. Her response was, "Look how it paid off!" Conversations happen all the time, and you will have multiple opportunities to say things in a variety of ways. As a bonus your child will have just as many opportunities to comprehend.

Explain often

Repetition is our friend as we pepper our conversations with the who, what, when, where, and why of daily life. Use every opportunity to explain and expand upon the subject for the benefit of the listener. If you are using applied behavior analysis (ABA), you can infuse explanations. For example, if you are teaching your child to say "hi," you can introduce each session by giving a brief explanation of why we greet each other. (Another good use of multiple opportunities!)

Use questions

Intersperse your conversation with questions and wait for a response. If you're talking about your child's school day, ask simple questions, "What color did you paint the dinosaur?" "Did Emma come to school today?" On your drive home, you see a pedestrian walking a big dog. Ask your child if he likes big dogs. Let the questions fit into the day's circumstances. Depending on your child's abilities, you may or may not get a verbal response, but this shouldn't deter you from practicing a conversational mode. Although we don't know the child's thought processes, we've set up the framework and cadence for conversations and have provided opportunities to reciprocate, even when the answer is void of words. Imagine the delightful opportunities you have when you do receive a verbal response!

Model a response

If there are holes in your conversation where the other participant would normally step in, play the participant's part after waiting long enough for a response. For example, you ask your child, "Do you think the cat wants a treat?" You wait about five seconds, and if you don't get a response, you say, "Yes! The cat is scratching at the treat cupboard. Let's give her a treat!" Questions for those with ASD can be especially challenging because of language processing difficulties, so modeling the answer is an effective instructional tool.

Verbalize your thought process

You may be surprised that you, too, are benefiting as you solve problems or gain understanding simply by changing your thinking process from internal silence to verbalization. You make multiple decisions per day, and if you verbalize them—for example, what are you doing for dinner tonight?—you will be modeling an important skill in a natural setting. Your *aha!* moments will be shared events that you co-create with your child.

Assign meaning to movement and intent

Remember, a response can be verbal or *nonverbal*, not verbal or *silent*. Be on the lookout for your child's nonverbal responses: an upward glance, body movements, coming just one step closer. You may notice your child opening his mouth in preparation to speak, even though he maintains silence. Your child intends to communicate and, as you respond, you strengthen the connection. Nonverbal communication *is* communication.

Use read-alouds as a springboard

Read to your child daily and continue doing so beyond the primary years. Words from a book jump off the page to inspire conversations about your child's favorite topic both in fictional and informational texts. Many children on the spectrum who are fluent readers still struggle with comprehension, so your guidance over the years will support your child's understanding of his world.

Conversations are naturally occurring events that have the immediate effect of creating a connection and making sense of the participants' worlds. You needn't worry about saying the right thing or getting professional results. Simply by engaging in conversations with your child—verbal or not—you are respectfully giving him the human connection that everyone needs and deserves. You're not alone. Many others, including your child's speech-language therapist, participate in your child's world to help him create the human connection through communication.

The speech-language therapist's role

In my world of service providers for children with ASD, I imagine the speech-language therapists as the ones wearing armor, riding in on their strong horses. They are frontline champions who help parents begin to make sense of their child's communication challenges. Because delayed language is usually one of the first symptoms that parents notice, speech therapy is recommended for the child often before a diagnosis of ASD is confirmed.

Parents receive advice freely from family, friends, and neighbors about their child's speech delay. "Enjoy the silence now. As soon as he begins to talk, he'll never be quiet." "Einstein didn't talk until he was five." "Boys always talk later." I wonder if these same advisers would be as patient waiting years for a lower-level human need, perhaps a delayed paycheck. Communication is one of the most basic needs for independent survival, and speech-language therapists understand the urgency for intervention.

Unless exposed to the profession, people could think that the purpose of speech therapy is limited to helping children and stroke victims with pronunciation skills. The parent of a nonverbal child doesn't understand how a speech-language therapist can improve the pronunciation of a child who doesn't talk. Likewise, the parent of the verbal child won't see a need for speech therapy when every word the child speaks is understandable. This view limits the therapist to the *speech* portion of the profession where the production and sound of speech is addressed. Sometimes children with ASD need guidance with the production of speech, especially if they have apraxia, a motor speech disorder where the child's brain is inefficient in sending signals to the mouth to create understandable speech. Children with ASD, however, benefit from the *language* interventions received from the speech-language therapist that address the following needs:

- *receptive language disorders*—difficulty understanding others' communication (receiving/taking in language)

- *expressive language disorders*—difficulty expressing oneself (language output)

- *social communication disorders*—difficulty using verbal and nonverbal communication in social situations.

Your child's pediatrician may be the first to suggest speech therapy if, during one of your child's milestone checkups, she determines a speech delay. The ASD diagnosis reveals deficits in social communication and, again, the speech-language therapist is usually called upon for supportive services as a follow-up recommendation. If your child has an ASD diagnosis, he most likely has an IEP, and should qualify for speech therapy services, at no cost to the parent, in the school setting. Don't stop there. I've seen young children make excellent strides in communication skills when they received both school and private speech services. With more states mandating insurance coverage for ASD services, and with the help of government assistance, many more children can receive private speech services.

Speech-language therapists share their knowledge with parents to educate them and recruit supportive help. When the parents understand the purpose of the therapies, they can help the child practice new skills in everyday settings, not just in a therapy room. Ask the therapist for clarification if you are not sure of the goal, and report back with how your child is progressing at the beginning of each session. Your collaboration will increase your child's chances for positive growth.

Communication at school

Parents of five-year-olds worry about how their child will adjust to the demands of the new kindergarten setting. Parents of children with ASD worry with fervor, especially when they consider communication challenges. They are concerned about receptive language—will the child look insubordinate if he doesn't understand the teacher's instructions? Expressive language deficits cause apprehension, too—how will the child say when he needs the bathroom, or tell a friend he wants to play?

Parents can ease their concerns by contacting the child's teacher before the school year begins, as suggested in Chapter 1, "Kindergarten Transition and Placement." When the teacher understands beforehand that your child has expressive and receptive communication challenges, she will be much less likely to misinterpret his intent. You can let the teacher know how your child communicates and what supports he needs/uses. On occasion, the kindergarten teacher isn't identified until the first day of school because of staffing procedures. Instead of sending your child into that potential chaos, strongly consider sending him once you have had the chance to talk to the teacher. You want the first day to be a positive one, even if it is the second day for all other students.

Your child will be in a variety of settings at school and will need communication skills in each one. Use the strategies that have worked so far, and get ready to incorporate new technologies and methods to meet the communication needs in your child's school environment.

Augmentative and alternative communication supports

Humans talk because we can. No other species has the physical attributes and brain structure that make us the sophisticated, rapid, and efficient communicators that we are. Sometimes an anomaly of nature changes the communication system, as we see with ASD, so we accommodate with varying supports.

Augmentative and alternative communication (AAC) does what it says. It *augments* oral speech and offers *alternative* ways to communicate. It comes in many forms, ranging from facial expressions, to the use of pictures, to writing or keyboarding, to speech-generating devices. AAC effectively supplements existing speech, and it can produce speech/communication for the person who cannot do so with his own voice (Beukelman and Mirenda, 2012). You've seen the frustration that your child experiences when he cannot express his wants, needs, and desires. AAC flexibly helps your child's communication skills.

Kindergartners who need AAC use a variety of interventions with ease once they've been trained on the system that is selected as best for them. AAC interventions rely on the visual expression of communication with pictures for the younger child. I've observed over the years how quickly children respond to a picture as compared to a simple sentence or even a single word. Compare it to humor: a spoken or written joke requires the receiver to use complex decoding skills to find the funny. Add a picture to the joke and comprehension becomes a little easier. Show slapstick humor, and you get immediate laughs. The same chain of events occurs with communication in general. The visual representation is processed more quickly because it requires the least amount of decoding.

AAC offers a variety of methods to help the child with expressive language, and the speech-language therapist usually takes the lead in recommending AAC interventions suitable for your child. AAC gives the child the opportunity to express himself more quickly and effectively by using any of the following interventions.

Sign language

Parents and teachers can pair words with signs to enhance receptive communication, and the child can use sign language to express himself. Sign language is with you wherever you go! I use a limited amount of signs in my classroom, but I use them often throughout the day. My students use the same signs to communicate, especially for *yes, no,* and *more.* The speech-language therapist can recommend the extent of sign language the child learns. When the child learns to sign, it follows that those who communicate regularly with him will need to learn in tandem.

Picture Exchange Communication System (PECS)

The child exchanges a picture for a desired object. Through using this system, the child learns communication basics such as joint attention with his communicating partner, how to engage in social interactions, and how to take the initiative as a way of advocating for his needs. PECS works by using a series of pictures on a board or in an app for electronic devices as choices for the child. For example, a child would have a strip with three pictures that represent the day's choices for a snack. The child gives the picture of his snack choice in exchange for the actual snack; or the board could include an open-ended sentence: "I want _____" where the child attaches the picture of his choice. PECS is produced by Pyramid Educational Consultants, Inc., and is included as one of the 27 evidence-based practices for children with ASD (Wong and colleagues, 2014). The child's speech-language therapist works with the parents and teachers to implement and expand PECS for the child.

Speech-generating devices

Also known as voice output communication aids, this technology produces speech quickly for the user as it speaks words or phrases when a picture or symbol is touched. The typical speech-generating device is a stand-alone unit about the size of a tablet but is thicker, heavier, and sturdier. The programmable device accommodates the child's growth through increased levels of usage beginning with a few pictures and expanding to several categories. My nonverbal student who was not successful with other forms of AAC started with four pictures on his device and learned to use them appropriately to communicate. The speech-language therapist increased his choices as he showed comprehension of more vocabulary. The child's communication with a speech-generating device is so authentic that I forget I am receiving words in electronic form. I smile when my student expresses what most children want to say a half hour before dismissal, "Go home!" Even with limited speech selections, children learn to express their needs. One student combined "bathroom" with "mommy" while showing a desperate expression. The adults quickly realized he was sick and needed immediate attention. The speech-language therapist assesses the child's communication needs and makes the recommendation for AAC on an individual basis. Speech-generating devices tend to be more costly than other AAC interventions.

Applications for electronic device

Numerous apps for smartphones and tablets have been created that offer generic supports for communication for those with ASD. The apps give picture support for communication and sometimes mimic the strategies of PECS and speech-generating devices at much lower prices. You can enter "autism AAC apps" in your search engine to review your choices. Before you purchase, consider two things. First, have a conversation with your child's speech-language therapist because you want the right fit for your child's communication needs. Second, tablets and smartphones contain more than the AAC apps you purchase, and our tech-savvy youngsters can exit any program to find the more entertaining games. Your AAC app purchase has the potential of being actively ignored or minimally used.

In your search for interventions that will help your child communicate, you may have come across *facilitated communication*, a method where a facilitator guides the hand of the person who has a communication deficit to type on a keyboard or point to letters. The American Speech-Language-Hearing Association (1995) published a position statement indicating that most facilitated messages originate from the facilitator and not the disabled communicator, and that facilitated communication has yet to be proven reliable. We want our child's communication to be authentic, without the risk that a facilitator is creating the message in lieu of the child.

AAC promotes independence, self-advocacy, and the human connection. The speech-language therapist guides the child's communication growth with regular therapy appointments and also offers training to parents and educators on the use of AAC interventions. When you first learned about the communication challenges of ASD, you probably felt as if you lost your footing. Now, with the support and practical interventions of the speech-language therapist, you're marching on solid ground to the steady beat of communication growth for your child.

Social communication

No matter where we are, we communicate to make connections, and the school day offers multiple opportunities for social communication. The child's social circle begins with his classmates and teacher; then ripples out to the music and art rooms, the gym, library, and cafeteria; expands its edges to recess; and stretches out even further on field trips. The adults have many chances each school day to be the interpreter and converser as they guide the child with ASD to take part in social situations. Consider sharing the ten pointers listed earlier in this chapter in the section "Creating opportunities to connect," with your child's teacher so she, too, can help make the anytime/anywhere connection with your child.

Please refer to Chapter 7, "Social and Emotional Growth," for an in-depth discussion about how children with ASD learn social skills and strategies that are effective in a school setting.

The role of communication in learning

Welcome to my three-step school where I delight in your desire to absorb new information and make it your own! Don't worry about bringing any supplies or books; I just need you and the three steps:

1. Joint attention

2. Receptive language skills

3. Expressive language skills.

You're set to go. But what about your child with ASD? Can he attend the three-step school even though he brings only small portions of each? Of course he can! Look again: I said I need you and the three steps. You provide yourself; I'll work on supporting the three steps. After all, I'm the teacher here.

When you send your child to school, you don't think about learning as a function of communication. It's just learning. It's what all kids do when they go to school. Scientists can explain how the brain whirrs and pings like a pinball game when engaged in learning, and we can find the path to light up the brain's learning centers when we support joint attention and receptive/expressive language skills.

Joint attention

Social communication begins with joint attention. The pinball begins to roll when the student and teacher achieve joint attention, which consists of three parts: orienting, sustaining, and shifting attentions.

Orienting attention

You request the child's attention and then expect to see his initial physical adjustment as he looks at you or walks toward you. We actually are asking the student to transition, and we know that can be a challenge for a child with ASD. Students transition best when they are prepared—the earlier the better. My students know the schedule of events before the day begins. In fact, these five-year-olds bypass their lockers in the morning to make a beeline for the schedule board, just like we check out the headlines of the daily paper before diving in. Some will even go to their personal visual schedule to see when their breaks occur. I've given up on my rule, "first locker/then schedule"! They've shown me which priority is highest.

Even though a child has foreknowledge of a transition, he can still struggle in the moment to orient his attention when the request is given. We can't always determine why the child has this difficulty, but we can accommodate his struggle. When making the request, place yourself in direct view of the child. One of my student teachers told me that Chase won't come for his lesson. I watched her call to Chase across the room several times, yet he didn't acknowledge the student teacher. I explained that teachers beckon their students actively, and that she needed to walk toward Chase, allow him to see her, and then deliver her request for attention.

You can strengthen your verbal request for orienting attention by pairing it with a visual support. I make several requests for students to physically orient to the lesson, both to get them where they belong and again to regain their attention mid-lesson. Some students require an enticing visual, such as a wooden train engine, while others respond to a cue, perhaps an object from the lesson. I never use an electronic device or book with sound buttons as motivation to orient. You know how that story ends!

When I run a systems check for the green light to teach, the first thing I want to see is a student in his seat. I'll occasionally complete a lesson while allowing the child to stand for part of the time, but my goal is to help the child prepare for his next 12 years of education where, realistically, he will be seated for his lessons. Sometimes it takes a good portion of the kindergarten year to teach a child to orient by sitting for a lesson. Teachers can give more individual attention to the child in a small class, but when the child with ASD is in a room with 20 or more other kindergartners, the task of gaining attention can be more difficult. Your child's teacher will tell you that he walks around the room instead of going where he's supposed to be, or that he doesn't participate in circle activities. I've observed this scenario, which reminded me of when I took driver's training on a simulator. They switched us over to stick shift, and I sat there at my stalled simulator while watching the car move through town on the big screen. So it is for the child in a larger classroom: if he can't orient, he watches the act go on without him. Ask your child's teacher to observe the first step of orienting when she tells you he isn't paying attention or participating. Before trying to fix anything else, find out if the child simply stalled out.

Sustaining attention

Now that Chase is seated for his lesson, I want him to sustain his attention. I look at Chase, he looks at me. I'm ready to begin the lesson when Chase points his finger at me.

Are you okay?

Yes, Chase, I'm okay.

Are you okay?

Yes! Are you okay?

Are you okay?

Chase's perseveration and echolalia trumped my introduction to the lesson. Sometimes Chase will give his attention to his perseveration and sometimes I can detour him toward the lesson. My first priority, however, is to obtain and sustain Chase's attention. No matter what subject he's learning, my primary focus will be to improve Chase's joint attention.

Those with ASD sometimes will avoid or resist human interaction, which influences the length of time they can maintain joint attention. To increase the time we stay on task, I incorporate the students' favorite themes and add visual prompts. I've learned to gently persist when seeking joint attention with my students yet, at the same time, tolerate the attempts it takes to gain it. Just as we do when conversing with a child with ASD, we take advantage of multiple opportunities.

While juggling the current lesson with attempts to keep the student on track, I try to find indications of my student's effort to sustain attention. It's in these little cracks that hope springs up. The student shifts his eye gaze toward me for a second; he picks up an object related to the lesson; or he simply stays in his seat without darting away. I always acknowledge these efforts and use positive reinforcement to encourage encore performances. Old-fashioned paying attention is hard work for my students and I honor their efforts.

Shifting attention

After all the effort the child put into sustaining attention, we ask him to shift it! We need our students to be able to disengage from a current activity and reorient to a new one. In a learning situation, we switch modes to demonstrate, work on the interactive whiteboard, or fill in a worksheet. When the lesson's structure is predictable, the student can anticipate the transitions and reorient without a struggle.

Not all lessons follow the same structure day after day, and not all students have the capacity to disengage and reorient. I try to prepare the student for mini-transitions within a lesson both verbally and visually. After giving a verbal one-minute warning that we will be switching activities, I use a visual timer so the students can see the minute dwindle away. If a timer isn't available, I tell them we will switch after I count down from ten to one (slowly). When I inform the students that it's time to switch activities, I either begin to clear some of the lesson materials, or I add objects that we will use next— all to support shifting attention.

Joint attention—the desired outcome

I look at the bigger picture when I work on the three parts of joint attention. Certainly my students are more attuned to their lessons when they can orient their attention, sustain it, and even shift attention midstream. I treasure the moments when my students are absorbed in learning, when the world drops to the background and time stands still. Teachers live for this experience.

Those of us who teach children with ASD live for it even more. When a child increases his ability to jointly attend, he is spending time actively engaged with another human. He's not alone; he's made the connection! Because of this, he will increase his chances of gaining language skills. This is the big, beautiful picture!

Receptive language skills

Learning begins with receiving. You receive a traffic ticket; you learn to drive the speed limit. You receive a compliment; you repeat the action that got you praise. You receive new information; you process it. We're presented daily with myriad informal learning opportunities through print and electronic media, relationships, and observations. The presentation of formal learning, however, tends to be confined to the spoken and written word. Kindergartners depend entirely on the teacher's spoken words to learn academics and classroom expectations. They have only one main channel to receive instruction.

The language-rich environment

Try to imagine what happens when a child with a receptive communication disability is spoken to. We can't see his thought process, specifically the areas of his brain that burst with activity, or where the message is stuck or incorrectly routed. We just see a confused or anxious youngster. Once the child receives the communication, it's out of our hands. When the child responds, the receptive process is complete and he's moved on to expressive language or a physical response. We can't go where the receptive language problem is occurring.

We face a conundrum: the child has difficulty processing language in a language-rich learning environment. In my years of experience, the most effective intervention is to use language.

Kindergartners are assessed for reading readiness as they prepare to take the steps toward literacy. Caldwell (2010) found that reading achievement is strongly tied to oral language development, listening comprehension, and the quality/amount of oral language interactions the child experiences at home before kindergarten. This means that our children with receptive language disorders need to develop, understand, and use language. We're back to the beginning of the chapter in the section "Connecting through conversation," where we give the child with ASD language and vocabulary-building opportunities.

The child with a receptive communication disorder may always deal with the challenge, but he can grow with it, too. At the beginning of the school year, a visitor asked my student his name and he replied, "five years old." A receptive language processing glitch occurred that was confirmed by the boy's answer. Throughout the year, I asked the same question and began to get the child's name after a delay of several seconds. By the end of the year, he answered correctly and quickly. If I didn't use my language with this child, he would have missed an opportunity to grow.

Adapting language for the child

We don't toss the child into the language-rich learning environment for a sink-or-swim experiment. Instead, we bring language to him in a form that is easier to receive with the help of time, visual supports, and measured communication.

Once the language leaves our lips, all control of the receptive process is with the child (but sometimes I think if I smile and look at my student with wide, expectant eyes, my words will land in a good place!). Teachers and parents of children with receptive language challenges know to give the child more time to respond. Not everyone knows this, though. People don't like a void, even if it's less than ten seconds, and will want to fill it. Classmates answer for the student, and cafeteria workers repeat their question if they don't get an immediate response. The teacher advocates for the child with ASD when she teaches everyone in the school environment to allow silence for language processing time.

Pictures help the student process language more easily because they require less decoding than spoken or written words. I make small visual signs with craft stick handles for the most used requests such as *wait, quiet, my turn/your turn.* While I'm teaching, I can continue the lesson and redirect a student simultaneously simply by showing the *quiet* sign. As with many interventions, the signs work with all kindergartners, not just those with receptive language disabilities. I add visuals to anything I want my students to comprehend: lessons, class rules, social narratives, even the lunch selection.

When I need my students to follow a directive or respond to a question, I use measured communication—the right amount of words to express the request. The right amount for one child could be one or two words, and a full sentence will work for a different child. I avoid being redundant or verbose, and I give the child time to process. Parents and teachers can hesitate to expand a child's capacity for receptive language, especially if they became accustomed to giving short directives when he was younger. Even though the child is nonverbal, he can grow in his capacity for understanding receptive language. Why continue asking, "George want juice?" when he could also answer the question, "George, do you want juice or water?" The child with receptive language challenges will grow in his capacity to process and comprehend language when he has the right supports in place and has daily opportunities to practice.

Expressive language skills

Expressive language allows the student to show what he knows in the learning environment. Kindergarten students use receptive language to absorb the teacher's lessons and employ expressive language to give feedback on what they've learned or where they need clarification.

Children with ASD often have both receptive and expressive language disabilities to some degree. Because expressive language is the output, we have a product to work with, or to entice out. We can be more active, so it seems, when we support expressive language. It's not as mysterious as receptive language where we don't see what happens once the words are absorbed.

Expression beyond words

Some teachers say, "Tell me what you know." My mantra is "Show me what you know," because all forms of expressive communication are valid. In addition to the spoken/written word, the child can express himself through:

- non-word vocalizations
- eye gaze
- facial expressions
- pointing
- physical movement
- leading an adult to what he wants
- drawing
- AAC: sign language, PECS, speech-generating device, apps on electronic devices.

A child indicates that he can successfully initiate a response when he shows *any* form of expression. From this starting point, we teach him how to expand his expressive communication. Think back on one of your most-used words as you described your child during the diagnosis process. "He seems *frustrated* all the time." "He doesn't talk, and I think he's *frustrated* that he can't tell us what he wants." Frustrated indeed! The little tyke is showing us the immense importance of expressive communication in every setting. That's why the parents, teachers, and speech-language therapists collaborate to create channels of communication for the child with ASD.

Teachers accommodate the child's style of expressive communication. We don't give him a failing grade because his classmates completed a worksheet, but the child with ASD just pointed to the answers and there's no hard copy of his knowledge. When parents advocate for their child's expressive learning needs, they have the support and expertise of the speech-language therapist backing them up. Remember, too, that the IEP is a legal document that must be followed. If it doesn't include expressive language accommodations for your child, you can ask that it be amended to do so.

The reflection link

Something happens after receptive language and before expressive language—learning! Expressive language gives the teacher an indication of comprehension, but how did that happen? You learn by reflecting. We focus on receptive/expressive language, input/output, and in the process we can forget to give time and guidance for reflection. Everybody, at every age, reflects to learn. It's not just an exercise for the retreat house, nor is it just for the guru on the mountain top.

Bella is a second grader who made great strides in her kindergarten year with expressive communication. Her predominant forms were physical (walking out) and non-word vocalizations (screaming). We worked to get Bella's environment suited to her needs, set some parameters, and looked for her talents and strengths. She loved to draw blue skies, fluffy clouds, and sunshine—what a pretty, serene view for this agitated young girl. When she could draw, she was content. Instead of allowing Bella to draw during free time only, we incorporated drawing as a form of expressive language in her lessons. In truth, Bella's drawing was an exercise in reflection. She showed increased comprehension of literature through her pictures. At first, every picture had the obligatory blue skies, clouds, and sunshine. With guidance and leading questions to prompt reflection, Bella added the main character onto the green grass below. Soon she began to print the character's name. Bella's latest masterpiece depicted Papa Bear discovering the intruder Goldilocks, with the subtitle, "Mad. Go away." Her only prompt was, "Was there trouble in the story?" I expect that Bella will be able to transition from pictures to written expression only. She already showed us how pictures have bridged her use of written words through reflection.

The uninformed person might think that nonverbal children don't use expressive communication. It's there if you know where to look; and when you find it, you can help the child increase communication and decrease frustration.

Paving the way

Communication deficits in young children require serious, ongoing intervention from professionals and parents alike. Hats off to the parents who embrace their role as interpreter and converser; who schedule and keep speech therapy appointments; who advocate for communication supports at school; and who delight in the growth of their young child with ASD.

You're paving the way for your child to fully connect in this world, and to say "thank you" and "I love you!" along the way.

Social and Emotional Growth

Now is the time to find friends.

Two young explorers with ASD teamed up because of a common interest in engineering. They braved new territory, built log cabins deep in the forest, designed trains over rugged terrain and, just for fun, sat together on the back of a tiger. I have the photo to prove it. In fact, I took the photo during inside recess after we put away the wooden building logs and train track. My young explorers ended their playtime by returning the oversized stuffed tiger to the corner.

How pleasant it is to exchange a myth—that anyone with ASD prefers to be alone—for a truth. Friendships are for everyone.

Flexible friendships

Think back to your kindergarten friendships when you chased one another at recess and saved the best valentine for your best friend. These activities occurred naturally without the guidance of an adult, and they created memories that outlast any kindergarten lesson. You want this rich experience for your child, too.

Friendship hierarchy

Will your child's friendships look the same as yours when you were in kindergarten? Possibly, or they could be comparable, tailored to your child's social abilities. The child with ASD experiences delays in language and social skills that are necessary to form and maintain friendships. When we teach any new skill, we parse the components to introduce the steps one by one. Playtime with a peer can fall on a continuum of relationship steps.

In the same room

Some young children with ASD are too stressed to be in the same room with peers. I've seen them escape by running away or clinging to a parent. I've seen these same children grow by remaining in the room, yet distancing themselves as far as physically possible from their peers. Young children need to take the first step in forming friendships by being there, in the same room, and being okay with their peers' presence. The anxious ones who have difficulty tolerating other children will need a slow, quiet start. They do best when they are in a familiar setting and when the number of peers is limited to one or two. As the child's tolerance grows, you can expand his experiences by trying new places or introducing a few more peers.

Playing side by side

You may have heard the professionals refer to *parallel play*—playing alongside one another with minimal interaction—when describing how a child with ASD relates to his peers. I mistakenly thought this neutral term portrayed a second-best activity when I first learned about how ASD affected young children. That was then. Now I rejoice when I see parallel play because I know the child is on the path to connecting with friends. He is able to tolerate his peers and begins to pay attention to them. The child with ASD is becoming comfortable with the unpredictability of humans that may have caused him anxiety in the past—differing facial expressions, changing body movements, and voice variations during play. Side-by-side play promotes the next step in social interactions.

Using the same toy while playing side by side

I use toy magnets to attract one child to another. Not *real* toy magnets, but toys that act like kid magnets. My students loved the delivery truck stenciled with a famous store name, so I bought another. Two boys trucked throughout the room, crossed paths, and even followed each other for brief periods. Their parallel play had moments of shared play. The dollhouse, wooden train set, building blocks, and swings work well for side-by-side play where each child does his own thing with a peer while using the same object. This style of play allows the child to maintain a feeling of safe independence as he grows in his ability to form friendships.

Sharing a toy

The act of playing side by side with the same kind of toy morphs into sharing a toy, a subtle yet important step in developing a friendship connection. When the child with ASD shares a toy in play, he is sharing attention. (See Chapter 6 on "Communication and ASD" for how shared attention is the most important first step in relating and learning.)

The opening example about my young explorers took shape over two years. Nicholas appeared passive and uninterested as a kindergartner, and Dion needed the first half of his kindergarten year to feel safe enough to walk into the room without crying. I set the supports in place to encourage friendships, but I can't predict who will connect. Classroom friendships still surprise me. Nicholas and Dion spent most of their kindergarten year playing independently, but thanks to their shared interest in building toys, they made a strong friendship connection.

You can encourage joint attention by providing toys that are high on the child's interest list. Electronic games on a tablet can create a quick link between children. I love the shared laughter that erupts each time the chicken didn't make it across the road in the silly app!

Creating play together

When you observe typical kindergartners on the playground, you are watching them create play together. The stick in the child's hand is a sword poking at the invisible dragon while the other children employ fight or flight strategies. Gottschall (2012) realized that the core of children's imaginative play is trouble, which helps them safely practice for life's challenges. Imagination can be frustrating for the child with ASD because of its abstract nature. I've not observed any of my students creating imaginative play independently. Some are able to follow the lead of their peers when the imaginative play is simple, for example, when they pretend to be zombies and chase one another. Objects, such as a dollhouse or puppets, can bridge the abstract imaginative play to a concrete item, increasing the child's comprehension of the play subject.

Group sports may not be the best match for young children with ASD. They may have to deal with motor development differences and can struggle with executive function tasks such as quick decision making. Think of the child up to bat at tee-ball. Was the hit a foul, or is the ball in play? Should he run to base or set the ball up again? Is he out at first or is he safe? All these decisions occur in a matter of seconds while the noisy crowd cheers him on. He's not going to be engaged in fun play when he is experiencing information overload. On the other hand, the child with ASD can team up with a friend to enjoy more individualized sports, such as swimming, biking, or bowling, as a way of creating play together.

As the child with ASD connects with peers, he also reveals weaknesses in his style. The unpredictable nature of his play partner can cause anxiety for the child with ASD, which he remedies by taking full control of the play. He probably won't be aware that his peers think he's bossy. He reveals social developmental delays as he struggles to share items and take turns. Don't let this worry you. Instead, be pleased that your child is growing and can learn new social skills. He's already moved up in the friendship hierarchy to be engaging with peers.

Children with ASD, like all kindergartners, have their individual temperaments and degrees of introversion or extroversion. My student Marco, despite his anxiety, is fun and outgoing and loves to make others laugh. He initiated a friendship with Eugene, an introverted, kind student who seemed content to be alone. The connection began when Marco made a silly noise that caused Eugene to laugh. I lost count of how many times this exchange happened over a few weeks! Soon the two boys paired together at every opportunity, showing visible care and concern for each other. The child grows into friendships as his social skills allow. Sometimes it's the peers who provide the spark as Marco did with Eugene. The adults, too, can give a little nudge to move the child's social growth forward.

Finding opportunities to support friendships

Parents and teachers have full agendas where it's difficult some days to fulfill even the basic needs. Just when we think our schedules will burst if we add one more activity, we try to fit in friendships— because it's that important. ASD is a social communication disorder that deserves high-priority interventions. The speech-language therapist guides language and social skills development in formal settings, but we're on our own for guiding the child's friendships.

Parent-initiated friendship support

In the course of your family activities, you probably already offer bountiful social opportunities for your child with ASD. You go to stores, plan outings for the zoo, and visit family and friends. All promote relationships and social skills. You may need a different tactic to promote friendships specifically for your child. Typical children initiate their own friendships, which have a way of working into family routines. Kayla asks if Emily can tag along at the zoo; Chad has Daniel over to play and he stays for dinner; and someone is always planning a sleepover. The young child with ASD doesn't yet have the language and social skills to initiate his own friendships, and that's where the parents step in.

Parents can set up the friendship structure for their child with ASD by creating playdates—simple affairs that can fit into your schedule. Begin with these three easy steps:

1. Determine your child's comfort zone from the five friendship hierarchy categories:

   a. in the same room

   b. playing side by side

   c. using the same toy playing side by side

   d. sharing a toy

   e. creating play together.

2. Consult with your child's teacher and speech-language therapist for hints and insights.

3. Identify friends—classmates from school or extracurricular activities, neighbors, cousins.

Make plans to create a playtime that suits your child's social comfort zone; incorporate the insights from the teacher and speech-language therapist; get some toys or activities that will hold the children's interests; and seek a peer for play. Keep in mind that you want to meet your child where he is, *and* you want to see him eventually grow to the next social step. If he can tolerate having someone in the room, you'll provide that comfort level, and you'll look for opportunities to have your child play in closer proximity to the invited friend.

At first you need only one friend, one place, and one hour. The child with ASD is usually more comfortable in his own home where you can monitor the play and reduce distractions. Unless there is a tiff, you needn't be actively involved. Watch, though, for signs of fatigue or boredom and cut the playtime short by offering a snack or taking the visitor home. Everyone is more inspired to play again when you leave them wanting more.

As your child becomes comfortable with his friend, you can expand the relationship by taking them to a park or fast food restaurant with a play area (investigate beforehand to determine when the crowds are thin), or by inviting more children to join the fun. I told a counselor about an unsuccessful playdate, and she correctly guessed that I had an odd number of children present. She said playdates work best with even numbers so that no one is left out.

You will take on the roles of initiator, chauffeur, and snack chef to get your child's friendships in motion. I've observed my students' pre-arranged playdates became more spontaneous after about a year, and eventually they resulted in steady friendships. In our local support group, mothers tell me about encouraging friendships as their children attended middle and high school, but at this stage, they help them learn to initiate instead of having them depend on the parents to create the opportunities. Friendships are for everyone. The kindergartner who cannot yet initiate one will benefit from the jump-start you provide.

Teacher-initiated friendship support

Your child's classroom is a little community tucked into the bigger school village where everyone experiences companionship. Learning takes place in a social atmosphere, so it makes sense that the teacher is an educator *and* a social director. Each child varies in social abilities and temperaments, and each needs guidance from the teacher that extends beyond learning the classroom rules.

Just as parents do, teachers switch tasks quickly and often to help the child learn social skills. No one schedules teachable moments; we need to be ready when they occur. The classroom atmosphere supports opportunities for growth when the teacher consciously desires her students to gain social skills and friendships. This desire is expressed through observations, insights, groupings, modeling, and direct instruction.

In the midst of lessons and transitions, the teacher observes her students' social interactions to notice who is teasing, helping, pairing, giggling, initiating, or avoiding. She looks to see who is included or excluded. These observations lead to insights for day-to-day, even moment-to-moment social lessons and groupings that support friendships.

Without a formal lesson plan, the kindergarten teacher creates opportunities for friendship, supports the relationships as they form, and models interpersonal skills. The current educational trend promotes rigorous instruction and student success measured by high test scores with no emphasis on social skills. Regardless of any educational trend, children will always need the guidance of a caring teacher to help them take the next step toward social maturity.

Each teacher's method of promoting social growth will be as individual as she is and will be influenced by the identity of the classroom community, which changes with each year's roster. Parents do best to understand their child's social needs at school through effective parent-teacher communication. Report cards make mention of social skill growth only through brief or generic comments, and the quarterly parent-teacher conferences give a snapshot of the child's school experience that doesn't highlight social skills unless they disrupt learning. This is enough knowledge for some parents. For those with a child with ASD, regular communication with the teacher helps define the child's social needs and interventions. (Chapter 2 of this book lays out a plan that promotes manageable, efficient parent–teacher communication.) Parents expect the teacher to report social difficulties and, just as important, the teacher needs to report successful social interactions as well. Together we work for the upward trend on the social growth chart.

Supporting social skills

Scans reveal that the brains of those with ASD fall within the normal range and cannot be differentiated from the brains of neurotypicals. It's the wiring, not the structure of the brain, that influences socialization differences such as avoiding eye contact or preferring objects to faces (Grandin and Panek, 2013). These marked differences can contribute to aloneness and isolation from other humans unless we intervene—the sooner the better.

Teaching social skills

Social skills training is not part of the formal kindergarten curriculum, and most young children don't need formal training to do what comes naturally. Their ability to make social connections is intact. They receive citizenship training—how to use good manners, share, wait, and take turns—because they already made the social connection. The kindergartner with ASD is just stepping aboard the social train. His destination is the same as his peers, but he's relying on us to give him boarding instructions. We don't want him standing at the station alone, and for this reason, we provide social skills training suited to his individual needs.

Informal encouragement

The kindergarten teacher gives individual and group direction to her students in response to social events that occur throughout the day. The child with ASD may not fully absorb these mini social lessons for two reasons: first, he doesn't have the same social foundation as his peers; and second, the teacher needs to gain the child's attention, and the mini lesson could be over before the student with ASD shifts focus. We never know, however, when one of these mini lessons will take root. We want the child with ASD to have exposure to his peers, the social interactions, and the mini lessons.

Children with strong empathy, boys and girls alike, tend to take the initiative to look out for classmates who need a helping hand. I've encountered these caring souls in every kindergarten class from east to west. They notice and respond to another child's needs even before the teacher is aware of them. They fill in the gaps for the child with ASD as they kindly lead him to the right spot or direct him to get out his crayons.

My students have recess with their typical kindergarten peers and I accompany them to encourage social connections. Nate called me over so I could see that he was pushing my student on the swing. I saw two happy boys—Samson because he loved to swing, and Nate because he was proud to help. As I praised Nate for his kindness, his peers took note and became part-time helpers, too. Nate was particularly good at making an extra effort to connect with my students. I asked him to join Eugene who liked to drop pebbles into the storm sewer, and to play chase with Ryan. Sometimes Eugene would get up and walk away from Nate, and sometimes Ryan just didn't run. Nate persevered. I look with hope to Nate's future because he will be someone who makes a difference.

Social guides are abundant in the classroom, too, and take it upon themselves to be on the lookout all year for a child whom they perceive needs help. One boy with ASD lost a helper because he was enamored with her hair and couldn't keep his hands off. That's the only unfortunate outcome I've witnessed in peer support relationships. Ask your child's teacher to identify a helper. Even if one doesn't currently exist, the relationship is easy enough to establish once the empathetic partner is found. Request that your child be seated close to his helping friend to foster the relationship. Everyone benefits from this community-building alliance.

Formal instruction

C-a-t spells cat; 1 + 2 = 3; say *hi* when I say *hi* to you. Your child attends school the same amount of time as typical children, yet in those hours your child has more to learn. Take the three Rs and add social communication lessons. Your child will work hard as he is requested to gain skills that address a core deficit of ASD. We require more from the child with ASD than we do typical students without a deficit.

Effective teams find clever ways to cross over each professional's area of expertise to support social communication for the child with ASD. The teacher and related service providers write IEP goals which they are happy to share with the team. The speech-language therapist creates a goal for the student to increase his verbal interaction with peers and adults by initiating conversations. The teacher and occupational therapist incorporate opportunities for this child to initiate conversations to give him more practice in a variety of settings. The IEP team supports one another's goals to increase the likelihood that the student will have ample chances to learn a new skill within the confines of the limited school day.

The speech-language therapist formally teaches social communication through individual direct instruction and in social skills groups. (Chapter 6 in this book includes a description of the speech-language therapist's role to encourage social communication and related skills.) She will teach nonverbal skills (body language, proximity to others, eye gaze); conversational skills (starting a conversation, asking and answering questions, staying on topic); and friendship skills (greeting others, taking turns, empathy).

Social skills groups give children of all ages the opportunity to practice while they learn. The groups usually consist of children in the same age range, but skill levels can vary. Some groups are learning the same skills together while others have typical children participating so that a peer, in addition to the adult, can model the skill and interact with ease. The speech-language therapist at my school mixes her social skills groups with students who have speech-only IEPs and children with ASD. The neurotypical peers encourage the children with ASD and keep the momentum alive.

Speech-language therapists lead social skills groups in school and private therapy. Other professionals, such as school counselors, special education teachers, and mental health professionals use curriculums to teach social skills in groups. For my kindergarten students, I use the program *Teachtown*, which depicts social skills lessons embedded in cartoons specifically created for children with ASD, ages two to seven. It fits perfectly into our schedule ten minutes before lunch when the students' attention is waning. Each short cartoon focuses on one social skill and includes quick activities to support the main idea. I use the taglines from many of the cartoons throughout the day when my students need a directive or reminder.

The Conversation Train (Shaul, 2014) uses pictures of trains to break down and explain the art of social conversation. This book can be used by parents and professionals to coach a child through the steps and rules required to be an effective communicator. Although it encourages verbal communication, the pictures alone will captivate any train lover.

Sometimes you find a book that you keep pulling out for review or fresh ideas. *Big Picture Thinking* by Aileen Zeitz Collucci (2011) is one of those books for me. She explains central coherence, its effect on thinking and relating, and offers specific social skills supports. Parents and professionals will gain insights, ideas, and direction that we can customize for our young ones with ASD.

Our hard-working students are learning social skills, practicing them, and eventually, with much support, will incorporate the skills across many settings.

Social goals in the IEP

For a child to be diagnosed with ASD, he has to exhibit social interaction deficits. This core trait impacts the child's relationships in all settings. I advocate for including a social goal on the IEP because the child has a proven deficit that can be addressed in the social setting at school. We create academic goals because learning happens at school, and we create behavior goals because behavior impacts learning. We can create social goals that affect learning *and* support the child's future social success.

I read the child's diagnostic report or the school's three-year evaluation report to understand specifically how my student is affected by social interaction deficits. With this knowledge, I observe my student's social behavior in the classroom and at recess to determine where he fits on the friendship hierarchy. I create goals that go a step beyond where my student currently performs.

I wrote the following goal for Trey: "When Trey is at recess or has free playtime, he will engage in a shared activity with his peers for the duration of two minutes, with 60 percent accuracy." Then I held my breath. I noted in the IEP that Trey engages 0 percent of the time with his peers when he selects his play activities, and participates with peers for an average of five seconds when prompted by an adult. Trey showed minimal progress in the first six months of the goal, and then began to exceed his two minutes with peers, not daily, but regularly. I set up situations to give Trey the best chance of spending time with his peers, and he grew into our expectations.

Mikey received school and private speech therapy that included a weekly social skills group at school. He progressed from being mute with occasional echolalia to making requests and responding to simple questions. I checked with the school's speech-language therapist before creating my social goal for Mikey because I didn't want to duplicate efforts. I was thinking of having Mikey say *hi* to us in the morning and *bye* at the end of the school day. I knew I was on track when the speech-language therapist told me, "Each week in group we begin by saying *hi* to one another. Mikey has never done this." Mikey needed to make a simple social connection with others by acknowledging them with a greeting, and the classroom was the perfect natural setting for this to take place. With much prompting and support, Mikey said his mechanical *hi* and *bye*. At the goal's end, he needed two or fewer prompts to greet others. The IEP team continued to work with Mikey to expand his greetings for more spontaneity and to include the person's name.

Emily is a girl of a few words but is a prolific self-taught musician and artist. In December, amidst the noise of inside recess, I heard Emily playing Beethoven's *Ode to Joy* on the toy piano. She runs to the computer at every opportunity to create intricate pictures with the drawing program. We used her interests to help her become aware of her peers. Her goal stated that Emily would tell her peers about her drawings, or tell them the name of the song she was going to play for them. Not only did it encourage Emily to use her language, it got her in the presence of her peers. Maybe as an adult she will need to explain her creative process to the crowd admiring her work at the art gallery!

Social goals do what no other goal category can—they put the emphasis on leading the child a step ahead of where he is now in relationships. If we overlook the social goal, we also overlook the importance of addressing a core deficit of ASD. Every child has a starting point and can respond positively when we show interest and patience in their social growth.

Teaching emotions

I attended an ASD conference workshop, *Focus on Feelings: Teaching Emotion Understanding and Regulation* presented by Shana Nichols Ph.D. (2013). She counsels children and young adults with ASD, and one of her observations took me by surprise. Dr. Nichols said that some young adults with ASD don't understand their emotions and can't identify many beyond happy or sad even though they have average or better intelligence. This lack of self-awareness affected their well-being and interfered with successful relationships.

I approached Dr. Nichols afterward to ask for her insights on teaching emotions to kindergartners, and she encouraged the practice, especially to help them understand when they are anxious or worried. In retrospect, the stretch of time between a child and a young adult never seems long enough, so now is the time to set the foundation for young children with ASD to learn about their emotions. Dr. Nichols inspired my resolve to begin right away.

Teaching emotions in the classroom

I dedicate a bulletin board to *My Feelings*, which I change regularly according to events or lessons. Thanks to online resources from *Teachtown*, the social skills program mentioned earlier, I had access to pictures of the character's feelings labeled with the identifying word. I switch between highlighting one emotion and showing pictures of several emotions. For example, when we get close to a holiday, I showcase one emotion: scared for Halloween, excited for Christmas, and happy for Valentine's Day. At other times, I rotate a mix of three or four emotions for display. We reference the feeling bulletin board in our morning routine and try to tie it in to the day's events. A student is *happy* because he has computer free time on his schedule, someone else is *worried* that the rain will turn into a thunderstorm, and another is *proud* that he could read the days of the week. I use the emotion pictures for spontaneous lessons, too. When my student throws himself to the floor because another child got an object he wanted, I point to *frustrated* on the board and say, "Tony, I see that you're frustrated because you didn't get the truck." That simple statement causes the child to refocus and identify his emotion in the setting. From there, the scenario can have several endings, but at least we got an emotion identified in real time.

Emotions and reporting behavior

I explain in Chapter 8 "Behavior and Sensory Support" that the behavior management system of green/yellow/red used by most schools does not serve our students with ASD. If you're good, you stay on green; begin to disrupt and your marker goes to cautionary yellow; and all is lost on a red day. This system teaches that we take things away when students display undesirable behavior, and young children respond just as you'd predict when you take something away. I needed a more effective approach.

I replaced the punitive green/yellow/red chart with a "Today I am feeling…" chart showing three simple, round-face choices: good (smile), okay (straight-line mouth), or sad (frown). Instead of reporting a green, yellow, or red day for the parents' daily communication sheets, the student selects an icon that sums up his day. Good represents a productive day where the child followed the rules and participated in lessons. His day was okay when he needed some reminders to share, keep quiet, or keep his hands to himself. When students have an okay day, I remind them that everyone has an okay day now and then, and we can try again tomorrow. The sad day rarely occurs, but when it does, I explain that it makes the child and others sad. The teacher is sad that she got bit; the student is sad that he cried and ran away from lessons. "Sad" describes an emotional response to the child's behavior as opposed to inferring that the child is "bad" because his color was moved to red. My goal is to teach emotions without judging behavior.

By mid-year, students begin to select their day's emotional measure independently. Most days are good days. Students have no fear to be honest with themselves to select the okay day when it is warranted. In the old system, they would cry and hesitate to circle the yellow while they experienced the pain of loss all over again. Now they have a better understanding of their emotions with knowledge that they can always try again.

Products to support teaching emotions

My students have learned to identify a variety of emotions with *The Transporters* DVD, a program developed for two to eight year olds with ASD. The eight *Transporter* characters are animated toy vehicles with human faces that captivate my students. Each episode includes quizzes that help the child identify emotions. Whether watching as a group or individually on the computer, my students don't tire of *The Transporters*, and the repetition serves to reinforce emotion identification and understanding.

Be sure to take advantage of your local public library's resources. The library can provide you with a wealth of books and videos designed to teach emotions to young children. You can try out the materials, keep your child interested in the variety, and sometimes discover a gem. I purchase my own copy of library offerings once I've had the chance to try them out for free. It could be the book that best explains what I'm looking for, or a video that my students want to see again and again.

Our young electronic wizards can use apps on the tablet or smartphone that are created to teach emotions. Every app collection for a young child should include an engaging emotion-identifying app.

Incorporating emotion lessons throughout the day

Opportunities abound throughout the day to identify an emotion. How does the child respond when the game device runs out of power, the cookie falls to the floor, or grandma comes over for a surprise visit? These events cause an emotional response that take just a moment to identify. The brief encounters add up over time to teach emotional awareness in authentic situations while repetition solidifies the learning.

Comprehension of literature relies on the child's understanding of emotions. *The Three Little Pigs* would be no fun for the listener if he wasn't able to detect worry, apprehension, and fear. Every story provides emotion-identifying lessons that teachers and parents can help the child understand. As an extension, story in any form—cartoons, movies, video games—has characters that show emotions.

You might be identifying the emotion for the child, or perhaps the child can identify some emotions independently. We're working toward the goal of comprehending emotions that supports both literacy and everyday life.

A positive impact

Everyone needs guidance in childhood to achieve social and emotional maturity as an adult. Parents and teachers of children with ASD focus their lens to find opportunities to support friendships, social skills, and emotional understanding. The entire universe existed above us centuries ago when Galileo invented the lens that allowed us to gain entrance into the mysterious mass. The universe didn't change, but our understanding of it deepened. So it is with guiding children with ASD. They remain constant; we are the ones who change by focusing our lens to find every opportunity to help them grow socially and emotionally. We will work harder and ask the child with ASD to do the same because we know the positive impact it will have on his well-being, now and in the future.

Behavior and Sensory Support

Accommodate when necessary and teach new behaviors.

You envision your child's response to kindergarten as the school year approaches. If you let your imagination run freely, you might see him removing his clothes, biting the teacher, or playing in the toilet. You know it could happen, but you hope that it won't! Your anxiety meter zooms upward whenever you consider your child's behavior and sensory needs, especially in a new setting where he is separate from you.

You are sending your complete child to school, not just the polite or charming portion. In this regard, your child is entering kindergarten exactly as all others. Reports of misconduct in kindergarten are like earthquake predictions in California—it's not a question of *if*, but *when*. Every child can have a bad day. You worry for your child, however, because his behavior and sensory needs might produce many bad days. You're concerned that peers and educators won't understand his response to the environment.

Your child can survive (even thrive!) in school with two straightforward interventions: accommodate when necessary and teach new behaviors. Action plans (specifically, these two interventions) sharpen the focus and keep anxiety at bay when getting the report about your child's mishaps. Approach the conversation with these interventions in mind.

"Behavior" and "sensory" defined

The *Diagnostic and Statistical Manual of Mental Disorders* of the American Psychiatric Association (DSM) (2013) specifically notes the sensory piece for ASD, but it defines behaviors only as they are affected by diagnostic terms. Those with ASD show a wide variety in the degree of DSM-defined traits; not all children will have identical needs for behavior and sensory support.

Behavior

The DSM takes an objective look at behaviors as part of the diagnostic process since no medical test can confirm ASD. The first two sections of the DSM-5 (American Psychiatric Association, 2013, p.50) state diagnostic criteria with terms, and expand them with behavior examples as shown on the following table.[1]

DSM V Section	Terminology	Behavior
A—Social Communication and Social Interaction		
A1	deficits in social-emotional reciprocity, ranging from:	▪ abnormal social approach and failure of normal back-and-forth conversation ▪ reduced sharing of interests, emotions, or affect ▪ failure to initiate or respond to social interactions

---

1   The table is reproduced with permission from the Diagnostic and Statistical Manual of Mental Disorders, Fifth Edition (Copyright © 2013). American Psychiatric Association. All Rights Reserved.

DSM V Section	Terminology	Behavior
A2	deficits in nonverbal communicative behaviors used for social interaction, ranging from:	▪ poorly integrated verbal and nonverbal communication ▪ abnormalities in eye contact and body language and deficits in understanding and use of gestures ▪ a total lack of facial expressions and nonverbal communication
A3	deficits in developing, maintaining, and understanding relationships, ranging from:	▪ difficulties adjusting behavior to suit various social contexts ▪ difficulties in sharing imaginative play ▪ difficulties in making friends ▪ absence of interest in peers
B—Restrictive/Repetitive Activities		
B1	stereotyped or repetitive motor movements, use of objects, or speech	▪ simple motor stereotypies ▪ lining up toys or flipping objects ▪ echolalia, idiosyncratic phrases
B2	insistence on sameness, inflexible adherence to routines, or ritualized patterns of verbal or nonverbal behavior	▪ extreme distress at small changes ▪ difficulties with transitions ▪ rigid thinking patterns ▪ greeting rituals ▪ need to take same route or eat same food every day
B3	highly restricted, fixated interests that are abnormal in intensity or focus	▪ strong attachment to or preoccupation with unusual objects ▪ excessively circumscribed or perseverative interests

The ASD diagnosis considers communication, social interactions, and restrictive/repetitive activities. I've had countless conversations with adults, including educators, who mistakenly believe that the third category is tantrums, not restrictive/repetitive activities. The DSM-5 does not use the word *tantrum* nor does its language describe behaviors that resemble one. Tantrums are available to any child who is overwhelmed! Look again at the table to note that the behaviors are generally calm and more complex than a tantrum.

The DSM-5 describes the effects of autism, but it doesn't describe your child. You know your whole child and you understand that, along with behaviors influenced by autism, he is learning how to maneuver life alongside his peers. So much behavioral learning happens at this age. All young children need to be taught to share toys, take turns, and say *please* and *thank you*.

Sensory

The DSM-5, Section B4 (American Psychiatric Association, 2013, p.50), defines one of the criteria for an autism diagnosis: "Hyper- or hyporeactivity to sensory input or unusual interests in sensory aspects of the environment (e.g. apparent indifference to pain/temperature, adverse response to specific sounds or textures, excessive smelling or touching of objects, visual fascination with lights or movement)." You think of things your child does that fit in this category: cries when he hears a siren, plays in cold water for a long time without showing discomfort, removes his shoes or clothes at inopportune times. It's difficult to imagine your child's inner reactions to the sensory world. We see only the resulting behaviors.

Many books have been written about sensory processing disorder (SPD), the brain's inability to take information gathered from the senses, organize it, and respond appropriately (Lashno, 2010). Occupational therapists lead the field in creating interventions for SPD through sensory integration, which also helps children with autism who have sensory challenges. The DSM-5 does not recognize SPD as a distinct disorder, stating a need for further research.

Therefore, your child's school district may challenge a request for sensory integration therapy or a sensory diet (individualized plan for sensory input activities) on the basis that they are unproven therapies. *Unproven* isn't synonymous with harmful or dangerous; many children benefit from sensory integration. Unproven therapies have been moved to the acceptable category through research; with the current rigorous research being conducted on SPD, we could see stronger support and advances in treatment. If your school district is reticent to provide services for SPD, refer to your child's *sensory input* challenges, a phrase from the DSM-5, to clarify that his needs are paired with his autism diagnosis. The team's occupational therapist should take the lead in designing sensory supports for your child.

Where to begin

As sure as the sun rises on your child's first day of kindergarten, he will need time to adjust to his new environment. The teacher, your child, and his classmates are busy finding a rhythm during the first few weeks. Two polar opposites occur in children's behavior at the beginning of the school year: they show their most challenging behavior and begin to relax as they learn the routines; or they show passivity and compliance at first, and reveal their struggles once they've acclimated. Unless your child's behaviors are putting him or others at risk for the first month of school, be patient as you monitor progress.

Your role as an advocate requires that you understand the complexity and delicacy of behavior growth. Strong sensory challenges can deter growth of any kind and require frontline interventions. Once the major sensory issues are calmed, the teaching of behaviors can begin. Spurred on by the child's improvement, enthusiastic parents can make the mistake of tackling the entire list of behaviors they want changed. Effective behavior changes are prioritized and measured, and take time for the child to assimilate.

If the right supports are in place, your child's progress chart will show an upward rise over time. Remember, too, that your child is learning how to adapt to his environment through osmosis while simultaneously learning the behaviors we are teaching. Honor your child's efforts and allow a pace that yields steady growth.

Now back to that call about your child's behavior… The conversation will have three parts:

1. the teacher talks and you listen;

2. you seek clarifying information; and

3. you discuss a plan to accommodate and teach new behaviors.

The middle of the conversation can be the trickiest. You may be trying to determine if the teacher is supportive, has no tolerance for variety in behaviors, or just doesn't know what to do. When the teacher and parent stay with the facts—what happened, what preceded the incident, how it was resolved—the conversation is more palatable than when emotional terms or generalizations are used. You don't want to hear that your child always shuts down because he is lazy, and the teacher isn't going to benefit from the parent saying that she is too high strung to teach a child like yours. Through teamwork, you and the teacher promote growth by considering how to accommodate the child's needs and teach replacement behaviors.

Ways to accommodate

Rarely will a kindergartner recognize that he is lost among the trees in an overwhelming forest, and even more rarely will he independently find his way out. The child communicates his response to the environment through behaviors, and the adults who know their way around the forest respond by removing fallen branches and hornet nests. We accommodate by making the environment suitable to the child's needs and consistent with growth expectations. The following are possible accommodations that help the child adapt.

Occupational therapy

The child's IEP team usually includes an occupational therapist (OT) for differing levels of support. Other team members may view the OT as the person who addresses fine motor skills for tasks such as printing, cutting, and gluing. While all team members agree that the student needs this support, the OT is the expert who is trained to understand the foundations of human development and the systems that support not only fine motor skills, but sensory regulation as well. The OT has a depth of knowledge and understanding that strengthens the IEP team and addresses the child's needs as no other team member can.

Your child's occupation for the next decade or so is that of a student, and an OT's core professional purpose is to help people participate in their environment (occupation) by acquiring skills necessary for engagement. The OT provides support for the student in his environment, the school, in the following ways:

Direct instruction

The OT assesses the child and uses the results to create interventions to support sensory input challenges and fine motor skills. She designs exercises and movements to help the student regulate his senses in response to how the environment affects him. She works with the teacher to implement suggested break activities into the child's schedule. The OT teaches the student how to grasp a pencil and use scissors and fasten/unfasten buttons, zippers, and snaps. The child receives direct instruction and individualized interventions from the OT to help him gain the needed skills to participate in the school environment.

Provision of support items

The child may need assistive technology to accommodate weak motor/coordination skills. Or, the OT might provide adaptive items to help regulate sensory input challenges, such as self-opening scissors, pencil grips, and a raised writing surface, to help the child accomplish tasks. The OT accommodates the student's hypo- and hypersensitivy issues, too. For example, the child who can't sit without wiggling or balancing the chair on half its legs may improve his ability to remain seated and attend to a lesson by using an air-filled seat cushion. Perhaps the child is calmed with a deep pressure or weighted vest. The OT understands the child's sensory dysfunction and selects the proper intervention items.

Consultative services

Some students may not have sensory input challenges that require direct instruction from an OT on a regular basis. The OT remains a valuable member of the team by being available for the child's occasional needs and by participating in the child's educational decisions. If a child has a change of behavior or drop in academic performance, the OT's input adds a perspective that otherwise might not be considered.

Staff training

The OT trains the staff to help implement the child's OT services included in his IEP. In addition to teaching the adults who are responsible for using the prescribed interventions, the OT educates support staff about the child's sensory needs. Cafeteria and office personnel, the school nurse, and perhaps even the janitor will have occasion to relate with the child. The child is best served when everyone understands his behaviors in regard to sensory input challenges.

Least restrictive environment

Chapter 1, "Kindergarten Transition and Placement," looks at where your child will be educated and discusses the least restrictive environment (LRE). The choice of a private, charter, or public school begins to describe the child's LRE; however, *where* in the building is he being educated? Your child can be in a large classroom with typical peers, in a smaller classroom where all students have special needs, or in a hybrid setting. Parents hope that their chosen placement works best for their child; but if he struggles in his current LRE, the team should consider accommodations contained in this chapter. If your child continues to struggle after accommodations are implemented, the team might consider a change of placement.

Instructional groupings

Your child's IEP may refer to individual or small group instruction in the *Accommodations* section. Many elementary classrooms incorporate different groupings throughout the day: the traditional whole group lesson given by the teacher; student-directed learning stations; small reading and math groups; and individual student-teacher conferences. These groupings enhance learning, but they may not be as effective for your child with ASD who has sensory processing and attention challenges. Many of the small groups in the kindergarten classroom require students to practice skills without the constant oversight of an adult, where the students use social skills and comprehension of spoken language to successfully complete tasks. With practice, your child with ASD can be taught the routines and benefit from these group activities. Your child also benefits when receiving direct instruction created specifically for him.

Small group and individual instruction for the child with ASD occurs with an instructor, usually a teacher (intervention specialist), and sometimes a paraeducator, and includes a lesson plan. These individualized lessons allow the instructor to teach and gather data for the child's IEP goals. Some students with more intense sensory and communication challenges do best with most or all of their lessons delivered individually or in a setting with a few other students. Others may receive instruction among their peers in a typical classroom, with a portion of the day's lessons delivered individually or in small groups. Many school districts have the intervention specialist go to the child's classroom instead of taking the child away from his peers for the small group/individual lessons.

The path to reach and teach the young child with ASD is a straight line—direct, individualized instruction delivered in a quiet setting. Children with ASD benefit from the accommodation of small group or individual instruction. The IEP team helps determine what amount of each type is right for your child.

Classroom environment

Effective classroom design provides structure, predictability, and consistency for students with ASD. It can support transitions and help students become more independent. It's a mix of what to include and what to leave out, what colors to use, and where to display instructional materials. In fact, an organized classroom supports the learning of *all* students. Many sensory challenges can be calmed with the right physical environment.

Parts of the whole

Regardless of the size of a classroom, it can have clearly defined areas including a place to take a break, independent work areas, group instruction areas, and a technology section. If the classroom has all these elements, but they are indistinguishable at first glance, the child with visual sensory processing challenges will be making more effort than his typical peers to follow directives and perform tasks. The teacher can create clearly defined areas by forming stations using bookshelves and inexpensive partitions, and marking off sections with tape.

Color and lighting

Kindergartners are learning the colors of the rainbow, but that doesn't mean the classroom needs a smattering of each color throughout the room. The simplicity of a main color with one or two supporting colors creates a calm atmosphere. Subdued lighting helps too, instead of the glare of overhead fluorescent lights.

Wall displays

Classroom displays for kindergartners should have the purpose of supporting the child's day. The schedule and classroom rules should get priority over the alphabet and numbers. Anything more might be too much of a good thing. I've seen kindergarten rooms with the entire wall space covered with papers, charts, and pictures. The child with visual sensory processing challenges will not be able to separate and distinguish each item's meaning, rendering each display ineffective and causing the child to be anxious. If the teacher has multiple displays, she can create order by spacing them apart and putting a border around each. Students' work can be posted in the hallway for all to admire instead of hanging among the other displays in the classroom.

Minimizing visual distractions

As your mother told you, *a place for everything and everything in its place.* Let's take that decluttering wisdom a step further: if it distracts, it must be addressed. The toys are neatly put away on the shelves, but oh how easy it is for a child to retrieve his favorite plaything in the middle of a lesson! Simply cover the shelves with a cloth—out of sight really is out of mind. If distractible items are too large to hide, such as computers or the teacher's desk, use visuals as a reminder of the students' boundaries. Signs of circles with the diagonal line, the international *no*, indicate blocked access. This worked particularly well with the computers as the students learned that access is available when the sign is removed.

Schedules and breaks

A schedule helps everyone—and is a *must* for a kindergartner with ASD. Even when the schedule of events remains consistent day after day, the students benefit from seeing it visually. A student teacher told me about a child with ASD whose teacher removed his schedule because he had it memorized. Yet the boy continually asked "What's next?" which the student teacher interpreted as the boy's intent to seek attention. He needed his schedule for the visual confirmation that reduced his anxiety. The teacher and student teacher were responding to the boy as they would a typical child, without understanding how perseveration affects a child with ASD and how a visual support calms the anxiety that it causes.

The schedule helps students stay on task, yet we know that the young ones with ASD are experiencing inefficient sensory systems, executive dysfunction, and learning differences. Within the day's schedule, students with ASD need breaks to refresh and to regulate their world.

If your child is experiencing shutdowns throughout his day, this could indicate that he needs a break sooner than he is getting one. What works as a break for most typical kindergartners—lining up for the restroom, lunch in the cafeteria, recess—doesn't always work for the child with ASD and sensory challenges. Your child refreshes when he gets several quick breaks that are scheduled and adhered to throughout the day. The few minutes away from instruction for a sensory break yields dividends as the child is able to increase his time in instruction without incident. The occupational therapist can suggest break activities tailored to the child's sensory needs that are engaging and fun for everyone. We take a daily two-minute break in my classroom for a yoga lesson on video that is scheduled in the afternoon when we begin to lose focus. When my students return to the room from an outside activity, we play a variety of quick games (ring toss, bean bag toss, three-pin bowling, a mini-obstacle course) and end with jumping on the mini trampoline. When I note that a student is struggling, I can have him interrupt his learning to help me carry a stack of books or take a walk to the office with me.

Exercise is an evidence-based intervention that is proven to reduce problem behaviors or increase appropriate ones. Keep this in mind when you think about including recess in your child's schedule. Children should not be disciplined by removal of recess, and teachers should not think the students are too busy for it.

Behavioral triggers

Sometimes you sidestep a child's nonproductive behavior by removing or blocking the trigger that sets it in motion. If a kindergartner melts down every day at lunch because of the noise level, and he continues to do so after using noise-reducing headphones, he might be allowed to eat in a quiet room. In this example the teacher removed the trigger—a noisy cafeteria—that caused the student to experience a high level of anxiety as a result of sensory challenges. You can block access as a way to stop an unwanted behavior, too. One of my students left his seat during lessons to run to the classroom's water fountain at least every three minutes, so I taped a plastic cup over the fountain to block access. No worries, all students still got a drink when they needed one. However, when the boy's destination was blocked, he was less tempted to perseverate on his routine.

The disciplinarian in us may want to avoid using the accommodation of removing or blocking triggers because we should require the child to learn what he needs to do. At this age, however, the child's bank of coping skills is far from complete, and some sensory issues don't fade over time. We prioritize the most important behaviors that our children with ASD need to learn, but as parents and educators, we recognize that lower-priority behaviors that occur simultaneously must wait their turn for direct instruction. We block triggers as a way of addressing disruptive behaviors that have not yet risen to the top of the priority list; and, for sensory needs, we remove triggers that cause excessive stress.

Sleep

We can't ignore the tired elephant in the room! Inadequate sleep affects the child's behavior at school. When a student puts his head down or falls asleep in his chair, I know immediately that he needs rest. It takes me a little longer to realize that agitated behavior is the result of sleep deprivation. After I redirect my student in quick succession a few times, I pause and understand that the child's behavior most likely is influenced by a lack of sleep. I can accommodate a tired child but learning will be at a reduced level on drowsy days.

Sleep difficulties are not uncommon for children with ASD, and parents' sleep is upset by the child who is awake in the middle of the night, too. If sleep issues affect your child's behavior and involvement in daily activities, his pediatrician may be able to offer a variety of suggestions to improve sleep. Regardless, when looking at the child's behavior, sleep should be considered as an influencing factor.

Ways to teach

Give me one week with a new student and I can identify three behaviors that interrupt his participation in academics or with peers. Give me another week, and I can pinpoint the behavior that most prevents the child from socializing or learning. How can I do this? I simply observe and take data! The behaviors introduce themselves as they come bubbling to the top, superseding all other actions of the child. Here is one boy screaming, "Mine!" as he wrestles items from his classmates; another standing with downcast eyes and drooped shoulders, resisting prompts to move to the table for a lesson; while a girl is fraught with anxiety and cries each time she is asked to show what she knows. The autism puzzle piece just got busted—we know the behaviors that affect our children's progress, and we know how to address the behaviors.

The child helped us identify the target, so now the team goes to work to determine how to teach new or replacement behaviors. We need to be aware that all interventions will belong to one of three categories that are defined by research data:

1. *Evidence-based*: scientific research proves the effectiveness of the practice.

2. *Unproven*: research for the practice is in progress but hasn't yet reached a conclusion, or the research was conducted by the creator of the practice with no confirmation of its effectiveness by researchers who duplicated the creator's study.

3. *Harmful or dangerous*: can cause physical harm or death; these practices tend to be biomedical.

After Wong and colleagues (2014) reviewed more than a thousand research articles, the team from the University of North Carolina, the Autism Evidence-Based Practice Review Group, qualified 27 practices as evidence-based. Most school programs select only evidence-based practices for their curriculum and methodologies. Some unproven practices are used for students, especially for sensory issues where research continues to study sensory processing disorder.

So many factors affect the child's behaviors: his individuality, age-appropriate development, ASD-related traits, and the influence of the cognitive theories (as explained in Chapter 5). We feel more grounded when we understand our child's behaviors, but even if we don't, we can still successfully teach productive replacement behaviors.

Applied behavior analysis

When people hear "applied behavior analysis" (ABA), they might envision a therapist sitting across from a toddler, giving him candy each time he responds correctly. ABA can look like that from an outsider's perspective, but let's focus on its central purpose: to improve behavior by using interventions based on the principles of learning theory (Alberto and Troutman, 2012). ABA is like a Swiss army knife where you pull out one cool tool after another.

While studying ABA for my license as a special educator, I was intrigued to learn that the purpose of any behavior could fit in one of four categories as explained by Alberto and Troutman (2012, p.172):

1. *Social attention*: behavior to gain the attention of others, including adults, peers, and siblings.

2. *Tangibles*: behavior to get a preferred object or participate in an activity.

3. *Escape/avoidance*: behavior to get out of doing something undesirable.

4. *Sensory stimulation*: behavior to feel good or satisfy a need (rocking, babbling, chewing items or clothing, smelling things, wiggling fingers in front of eyes).

While I take data on the behavior—when it occurs, how often, how long—I keep the four functions of behavior in mind. The purpose of the behavior helps me determine the best tool for the job. Consider how each intervention will be different according to the child's behavioral response to his environment.

Social attention

My student continually asks for adult assistance with independent work after he has proven to me in assessments that he can do the task on his own. I give him a timer to self-regulate and provide an opportunity to play a quick game of tic-tac-toe with an adult after he works independently for five minutes.

Tangibles

This is the most popular category in my entire career as a special educator! I've observed that students who intensely seek tangibles are also the ones who struggle with waiting and being told *no*. In this example, my student impulsively takes whatever he desires, regardless of where it is—on my desk, on the shelf, or in the hands of another student. I create social narratives that teach turn taking and how to ask for what you want. I also model the desired behavior and have practice sessions where I coach the child to act out the desired behavior.

Escape/avoidance

The second most popular category! Students can actively *and* passively escape/avoid. One student darts out of the room while another lays his head on the desk. For this example, we'll select the runner. I communicate the classroom expectations to the child in positive terms: lessons at the table, breaks in the quiet corner (where he's supposed to be, not where I don't want him going). I use positive reinforcement to begin building his desire to stay where he belongs. He gets a star for every minute he remains at the table, and after three stars, he gets a reinforcer. In time, the stars will be spaced out in longer intervals until we can fade the intervention because he remains in his seat.

Sensory stimulation

My non-speaking student continually vocalized "tat-a-tat-a-tat" during group lessons. Upon taking data, the vocalizations didn't occur when he had individual lessons or a break. The function of this boy's vocalizations during group time revealed that he needed this behavior when required to sit among his peers for a lesson. I seated the student a few feet away from the table, near an educational assistant, and gave him a string (his favorite item). By year's end, we moved him closer until he was sitting among his peers more quietly.

Notice how different each intervention is, depending on the behavior category we are addressing. I give attention in the form of positive reinforcers to encourage the child who is learning to not escape, and I encourage independence for the child who seeks excessive adult attention. I wouldn't want to use the same tactic for all behaviors or apply mismatched interventions that would be ineffective. This model helps you analyze the behavior and gets you closer—faster—to what the child needs to learn.

Positive reinforcement

Wong and colleagues (2014, p.21) define the evidence-based practice of reinforcement as "an event, activity, or other circumstance occurring after a learner engages in a desired behavior that leads to the increased occurrence of the behavior in the future." Let me translate that into a classroom situation. Jared is learning to stay seated. He gets a sticker of his favorite train character each time he meets expectations. Jared is motivated to get the sticker and figures out that he can sit for one minute. As he continues to earn stickers, he doesn't notice that he needs to sit a little longer for each one. As he approaches independence in this skill, his reinforcer goes from stickers to a high-five with the teacher. The positive reinforcement fades as the student learns the skill.

The first year I taught students with ASD, the school used the *green/yellow/red* system of measuring behavior. Good behavior kept you on green all day. If you had enough green days, you qualified for an end-of-the-month party. This may sound like positive reinforcement, but in reality, this system applied a negative consequence in hopes of decreasing future misbehaviors. When my students' color changed from green to cautionary yellow, they didn't stop to reflect about how to do better next time. At least, I don't think that was on their mind as they fell to the floor and screamed! Positive reinforcement occurs when the teacher *gives something* after the student performs the desired behavior, not when the teacher *removes something* after the student acted against expectations.

If your child has a cranky day at school, or comes home with a note saying his color was moved to red, check with the teacher about the use of positive reinforcement as a motivator to learn the classroom expectations and desired behaviors.

Modeling and rehearsal

When your child is learning a new behavior, it should be presented visually and in many arenas. Modeling allows your child to see the steps of a behavior correctly and more slowly than in real time. Modeling leads to rehearsal of the event. For the child who is learning to ask for items he desires, he can practice with classmates to ask for toys or books; he can rehearse by asking the paraprofessional if he can look at her charm bracelet; and he can practice asking for seconds at lunch instead of taking other children's food. Your child can learn to generalize the skill when he gets multiple opportunities across settings. Rehearsal is not a graded activity where you tell a child he passed or failed. If your child rehearses incorrectly, simply tell him to try again, and be ready to give pointers at trouble spots.

Video modeling is new to the list of evidence-based practices. Get ready for fun with this! Take your tablet or smartphone to record your student performing the behavior you are shaping. One of my students walked through the halls with his hands outstretched so he could physically feel every paper hung on the wall. (Not all papers survived.) I recorded him walking in the hall with his arms down—it took a few tries to get it right—and gave him verbal praise for a job well done. We watched the video recording before every excursion in the hall to reinforce the expectations. If the student touched the wall, I stopped him and we watched the 15-second video again. Eventually the touching was extinguished, but the student continued to watch the video during his break and smiled each time my recorded praise played at the end.

Social narratives

Social narratives became the generic term for Carol Gray's *Social Stories*™ (2010). They are short stories that describe the behavior you are teaching. You can find premade social narratives in books and online, but the most effective is the story that is tailored to your child's needs. The impact is increased when you add visuals, especially photos of the student and his environment. Make sure that teachers and parents share with one another the social narratives they create for the child.

I prefer to teach with social narratives when the targeted behavior isn't occurring so that the student has the chance to learn objectively and without stress. When you pair social narratives with modeling and rehearsing, you've provided the child with many golden opportunities for successful learning.

For the behaviors that are more rigid and don't show improvement with specific teaching methods, I go one step further and create the "prequel" social narrative. My student continued to shout "Mine!" and take objects from others after I tried to teach him how to share by employing social stories, modeling, rehearsal, and positive reinforcement. He didn't respond to all of the *hows*, so I looked for a way to deepen his knowledge. I made prequels to address his insistence that grabbing trumps sharing. Through the prequels, he learned what *is* his (my eyes, my shoes, my bed), what he likes, and if what he likes is his or someone else's. Once he understood these concepts, we were ready to try practicing sharing again. Sometimes we need to go backward to move forward.

Functional behavior assessment

A functional behavior assessment (FBA) is an evidence-based practice *and* is a tool recommended by the IDEA. A student is served by an FBA when his behaviors interfere with his classmates' learning, and the behaviors didn't improve after the use of other evidence-based interventions. Wong and colleagues (2014, p.20) outline the steps in creating an FBA:

- Systematically collect information about the interfering behavior.

- Describe the interfering or problem behavior.

- Identify antecedent or consequent events that control the behavior.

- Develop a hypothesis of the function of the behavior.

- Test the hypothesis.

Once the FBA is created, the child's team will create a behavior improvement plan (BIP) that states specifically how the needed behaviors will be taught.

IDEA requires a school district to create an FBA for any student who has a disability, has been removed from school for more than ten days as a result of a behavior, and has shown behavior that interferes with learning. If a child has been suspended for more than ten days, the behavior generally involves some form of physical aggression. An FBA/BIP doesn't need to wait for this level of drama. If a student doesn't respond to the evidence-based interventions that work for many, the FBA/BIP puts the behavior under the microscope for a closer look. I learned something new and unexpected about each of my students when I worked on their FBAs. One of my young students slapped others at random times without warning. Before the FBA, we focused on stopping the behavior. After looking carefully at the child's strengths and needs, and the antecedents and consequences of the behavior, we had a different plan. The comprehensive assessment showed us that the boy had a need for additional speech therapy to support communication, especially when he is frustrated. For those who still struggle after receiving evidence-based interventions, the FBA gives new insights on what you may have thought of as unreachable behaviors.

Planning for independence

We do more *now* for the child with behavior and sensory needs so that he can find independence *later*. We're building a skyscraper. Right now it's surrounded with supports and beams, cranes, and cement. The workers remove the supports when the building is fortified to stand on its own. Some of the supports, like the rebar inside the skyscraper, remain hidden in the structure. What we do now for the kindergartner with behavior and sensory needs will strengthen his future. It's well worth the investment!

Looking to the Future

Advocate now to lay the foundation for a positive future.

You're watching the kindergarten tree grow with its three main branches: your child (and the influence of ASD), the school experience, and you. The tree is getting fuller with outgrowths of friendships, social and communication skills, behavior supports, and academic learning. At the same time, you and your child are transitioning into new roles, and you're working harder than your average parent-child duo. You put forth the effort because you believe in your child's future.

Two transitions

While you're busy preparing for your child's transition into formal education, you might be overlooking *your* transition. Parents of children with special needs take on the role of advocate with zeal and without much help. Both you and your child have a learning curve to climb during the kindergarten year.

Your child's transition

Your child gives you indicators of how he is transitioning through signs of growth. Expect your child's progress in academic, social, and communication skills to be interspersed with rest periods that, when measured over time, show growth from point A to point B. Monitor your child's progress because it reveals how he is transitioning to formal education.

Your child progresses

You're receiving positive comments in your child's daily communication from his teacher, and the IEP progress reports and report cards give evidence of growth. All is almost well. Your child's behavior shows how he is handling the kindergarten transition, and that needs to be positive, too. Positive doesn't have to be perfect. Teachers look at baseline behaviors, those the students currently use to cope.

At open house before the first day of school, the parent of a new student told me that her son bites when he's frightened. Neil had the face of a cherub, the voice of an angel, and a sweet temperament to match. As predicted, he bit when he feared close contact that seemed unpredictable to him—helping him fasten his pants after using the bathroom, or guiding him to line up. We understood Neil's baseline behavior. If Neil increased this behavior to extend to his peers or to initiate a bite when no one was close to him, it would be a sign of regression. Neil's current, unchanging expression of communication doesn't cancel his overall positive progress because it's not an indication of regression. In time, we work with baseline behaviors to improve them, but their presence doesn't negate progress.

No progress, no regression

Parents and teachers might notice a lack of progress in an academic subject, or in social or communication skills. Often a child will stall in one area as he works to gain a new skill in another. For example, I expect minimal academic progress for the first month of school as the students practice classroom rules that will support learning for the remainder of the year.

We need to exercise tolerance and caution when the child's skill remains in a holding pattern. I tolerate one grading period with flat progress because I understand students' growth patterns of spurts and rests. I'm not concerned when the child's lack of progress is accompanied with cooperation. I become cautious when the lack of progress continues for more than one grading period, or when the student expresses anxiety or lack of motivation.

Dylan came to kindergarten with good academic skills but didn't make progress because of passivity that was influenced by his inability to initiate. He would stare at his schedule icon but would not proceed to the designated area. To support Dylan's transition to kindergarten, I incorporated interventions to help him learn to initiate. We need to determine if the holding pattern is influenced by a resting period, or by a challenging behavior or trait. The kindergarten year reveals needs that require support far into the future, and identifying the needs now promotes a positive transition.

The child regresses

As you read your child's report of regression, imagine that you're hearing alarms and seeing flashing lights. Something is impeding progress and disturbing the smooth transition to kindergarten. If the teacher hasn't contacted you, take the initiative to discuss the difficulty. Perhaps the level of learning needs to be adjusted to match your child's current ability. Parents know better than the teacher if a disruption at home could be affecting the child's participation in school.

If your child is regressing both academically and behaviorally, you have signs of an ill-fitted environment or a child in need of intervention, with either scenario resulting in a poor kindergarten transition. Act immediately to remedy the situation. Sometimes your child's IEP needs to be revised; sometimes more supports and modifications need to be added; and sometimes the placement needs to be changed. The sooner you investigate, the sooner your child can get back on track.

The kindergarten year influences the child's entire academic career. His progress will help guide your actions as his advocate.

The parent's transition

Parents go to open house to learn about school hours, attendance policies, and dress codes, but no one is teaching them how to advocate for a kindergartner with ASD. Instead, parents do their best to transition into the advocate role with on-the-job training. I've heard it referred to as "building the plane while we're flying it." I'm not a daredevil, and that's why I opted to write this flight manual! Check it often when you're concerned about communication supports, friendships at school, an upcoming IEP meeting, and the myriad of situations where you need a foundation of knowledge.

I've watched parents grow in advocacy skills while we worked through the challenges of kindergarten. Some worry that they are bothering me and might not initiate contact; some need more details than others about their child's day; and I've had a few experiences where I got the unrestrained version of a parent's concern. My friend told me about advocating for her son in kindergarten as she was learning to stand her ground. She told the principal, "You don't get it!" after she explained her son's need for gym accommodations three times. She knew immediately that she could have expressed herself better but, in the end, we all survive ragged communication.

Don't worry about how smooth you are as an advocate. The important thing is that you *are* advocating. Upon reflection, you may think you were too strong or too weak, or that you would do it differently. You'll get your chance to do it differently with 12 years of your child's education ahead of you!

Everyone's working harder

We've seen in the previous chapters how children with ASD have more learning packaged into the same amount of time as their typical peers. In addition to academics, we ask our children to expand communication skills, show social and emotional growth, manage sensory challenges, and learn new behaviors. Our diligent students with ASD deserve our respect for the effort they make daily to step out of their comfort zone in order to find their way in the world.

Parents understand that providing accommodations for a child with ASD involves trade-offs. I've known parents who delayed careers or opted to change from full-time to part-time employment in order to meet the time and emotional demands of raising a child with ASD. Parents simultaneously advocate for their child, coordinate appointments and services, educate themselves about ASD, and deal with the stress of raising a child with special needs. And don't forget all the other family, community, and work responsibilities waiting for attention.

Parents of children with ASD need support. Please find it in your family, friends, faith community, and support groups. Even with support, you don't live as you did before your child with ASD was born. Some things will slide. You'll go to bed with dirty dishes in the sink, and spring cleaning fades into a pleasant memory, never to be experienced again this decade. Your priorities changed while your obligations increased. Take an occasional breather to acknowledge that you're shouldering a serious responsibility; and keep your supportive relationships close.

Advocate today for independence tomorrow ▬▬▬

Ask parents what they do to support their young child's core deficits of ASD, and you'll get a full list of activities including speech therapy, social skills groups, and at-home interventions. Rarely will you hear parents tell you that they are teaching the child independence, yet they are. While parents do their job to help the child reach the next step, they simultaneously build the foundation for independence. When you begin to see adulthood on the horizon in middle or high school, your child will already have a strong footing with social, communication, and academic skills, thanks to your prior advocacy.

Immediate rewards ▬▬▬▬▬▬▬

In this garden of children (translation of the German word, *kindergarten*), you hope to see bountiful blossoms of growth for your son or daughter. Every child I taught gave me many opportunities to tell parents stories of progress. These successes give us strength to continue advocating and memories to cherish. I remember a special one from one of my parents. When the mother picked up her son, I told her that Kyle read books to his classmates during independent reading. The mother was overjoyed that he engaged with his peers by using his reading skills. On the ride home, the mother gushed, "I can't tell you how proud I am of you!" Kyle remained quiet the entire ride until she turned off the car. Then he asked, "Can you tell me now?" This came from a child who was mute just two years prior! Each success your child experiences will strengthen his ability to gain further skills toward independence.

Believing in the future ▬▬▬▬▬▬▬

Advocating is like a waterwheel, continually in motion with no definitive point of completion. It turns as your child settles into kindergarten; it turns while you lie awake in bed at night tired and unsure about the next step; and it continues to turn as your child succeeds and takes on new challenges. Your advocacy will power your child toward his fullest potential.

As you grow in experience and confidence as an advocate, especially after you've seen several cycles of your child's successes, you will still have moments when you ask yourself if you've done enough. The final lesson to learn about being an advocate is to believe in the future. Be assured from the parents who have gone before you that your efforts will bear fruit. When we plant an acorn, we await a sturdy oak tree. When we advocate for our child, we watch him grow—as the oak tree does—to the full potential of his being.

Practical Tools

PROFILE QUESTIONNAIRE (Part I)
Kindergarten Placement Checklist

Child's Name _____ Date _____

Completed by _____ Relationship _____

Skills for Kindergarten	Support Level			
	None	Some	Moderate	Intense
Self-Care				
Eats independently				
Dresses independently				
Toilets independently				
Communication				
Uses voice or communication device				
Responds to requests				
Initiates needs and wants				
Points to indicate knowledge				
Takes turns in conversation				
Understands pictures or sign language				

Skills for Kindergarten	Support Level			
	None	Some	Moderate	Intense
Socialization				
Plays with peers				
Takes turns in activities with peers				
Follows group directions (e.g. line up)				
Asks peers for help				
Responds to peer initiations				
Behaviors				
Waits quietly				
Transitions to new activities				
Shares (e.g. toys, games, electronics)				
Refrains from hitting, biting, kicking				
Participates in lessons and activities				
Remains in designated area				
Academics				
Identifies the alphabet				
Identifies the numbers 0–9				
Counts objects correctly				
Knows colors and shapes				
Reads and writes name				

PROFILE QUESTIONNAIRE (Part II)
Kindergarten Placement Fill in the Blanks

Child's Name _____ Date _____

Completed by _____ Relationship _____

Child's Strengths

Child's Interests

Successful Strategies

What else do you want educators to know?

TRANSITION TIMELINE
Fall (one year before kindergarten)

- Look into educational placement (with the help of the Profile Questionnaire):
    - Will you homeschool?
    - Will you choose a private, charter, or public school?
- If homeschool:
    - Get acquainted with homeschool parent groups in your area.
    - Visit your local library to inquire about homeschool resources.
    - Educate yourself for the job ahead by learning your state's requirements.
- If private or charter school:
    - Contact and apply.
    - Note: some schools require registration more than a year in advance.
- If public school:
    - Ask your child's preschool teacher what she envisions.
    - Contact your public school district's special education office to inquire about choices for your child.
- Private and public school choices:
    - Contact administration to inquire about orientations.
        - These can occur as early as November or December.

Spring (four to five months before kindergarten)

- Visit the classrooms of all considered choices.
- Finalize your child's kindergarten placement.
    - Meet the kindergarten teacher, if she has been identified, and get contact information for possible summer communication.
- If your child has an IEP, get a transitional IEP completed by May.
    - Keep your copy in a safe place.
- Before school closes for summer break, ask to take photos of the school, the classroom, the teacher, and common areas (cafeteria, gym, playground, art and music rooms, bathroom, office, nurse's station).
- Make certain the office at your school choice has your contact information, and confirm dates of open houses and first day of school.

Summer (one to two months before kindergarten)

- If homeschool:
  - Prepare your materials.
  - Meet with other homeschoolers:
    - With *only* parents to establish your place in a support group.
    - With parents *and* children to establish a social/learning group.
- If private, charter, or public school:
  - Take school photos on your tablet or make a book to acquaint your child with the new environment.
    - Review the photos/book regularly throughout the summer.
- Involve your child when purchasing school-related items (including new underwear and socks).
- Contact the school, the teacher, or the special education office with any questions or concerns that arise during the summer.
- Register your child at the school if you have not yet done so.
  - Visit the school with your child a week or two before the first day of kindergarten.
    - Contact the teacher or school to arrange a private viewing of the school and classroom.
    - Many teachers are setting up their classrooms before school begins and will accommodate your request to visit.
    - After the visit, view the photos/book again with your child.

PARENT/TEACHER COMMUNICATION CHECKLIST

Parent _____ Teacher _____

Method/Styles (Check all that you prefer)	Parent	Teacher
Communication notebook (reciprocal)		
Teacher note (one-way from teacher)		
Email		
Work (school) phone		
Home phone		
Cell phone		
Text		
Face-to-face (after school)		
Other:		
Frequency (Check your preferred method or rank your preferences)	Parent	Teacher
Daily		
Weekly		
Every reporting period		
Other:		
Availability (Fill in the blanks)	Parent	Teacher
Call as early as	a.m.	a.m.
Call as late as	p.m.	p.m.
Return messages/ emails within	___ hours or ___ days	___ hours or ___ days

INDIVIDUALIZED COMMUNICATION PLAN

Student _____ Date _____

Method(s)/Style(s)

Contact Information

	Parent	Teacher
Email		
Cell		
Home		
Work/School		

Frequency

☐ Daily   ☐ Weekly   ☐ Other: _____

Availability

	Parent	Teacher
Call as early as	a.m.	a.m.
Call as late as	p.m.	p.m.
Return msgs/ emails within	___ hours or ___ days	___ hours or ___ days

Signature of parent: _____

Signature of teacher: _____

CHECKLIST FOR CREATING THE IEP

✓	Task	Action
	Pre-meeting	
	Receive an invitation to attend an upcoming IEP meeting.	Sign the form and return the invitation to the contact person.
	Consider how you want to approach the meeting. Do you want an IEP draft in advance?	Inform the contact person about your pre-meeting preferences.
	Would you like anyone outside of the regular team to attend the meeting with you?	If so, let the contact person know in advance who will accompany you.
	Meeting	
	Each section is reviewed with time for discussion.	If not, ask to slow the pace or to reschedule when the team has time to review the entire IEP.
	Make certain the profile contains three elements: ▪ child's strengths and interests ▪ background information supported by data ▪ need for special education explained.	No action required if profile is complete.
	Parent's input is included in future plans.	No action required if parent's input is included.
	Goals are individualized to the child and are precise.	If you don't understand how a goal will be implemented, ask for an explanation.
	Look for precision and lack of ambiguity in these areas: ▪ related service descriptions ▪ accommodations ▪ modifications.	Keep the discussion going until the three areas are acceptable.

✓	Task	Action
	You and the remainder of the team disagree on services and cannot reach an agreement.	End the meeting without agreeing to the implementation of the new IEP and ask the administrator for a prior written notice.
	Participants indicate that they attended the meeting.	Sign the participants page.
	You agree to accept the new IEP.	Sign the section indicating acceptance.

CHECKLIST FOR IMPLEMENTING THE IEP

✓	Task	Action
	The current IEP is less than one year old.	Any IEP 366 days or older is noncompliant. Immediately ask for a new, compliant IEP.
	You receive progress reports for *each* goal on your child's IEP every time report cards or interim reports are issued.	If not, request progress reports immediately.
	Your child met one of his goals before the end of the IEP year.	Ask the team to reconvene to create a new goal.
	Your child is regressing on one or more of his goals for two consecutive grading periods.	Gather the team to consider changing the goals or the supports for meeting the goals.
	The child's behavior or social skills changed since the IEP was created.	Meet with the team to amend the IEP to reflect the changes.
	You get a call from the teacher to inform you of your child's negative behaviors.	Listen, acknowledge, and use the opportunity to clarify that your child is receiving all accommodations on his IEP to make sure behavior isn't a result of noncompliance.
	IEP services are not provided as you understood they should be.	First meet with the service provider. If not resolved, meet with the team.
	You and the IEP team could not resolve your child's noncompliant IEP.	Contact your state's department of education to learn how to file a complaint for noncompliance.

References

Alberto, P. and Troutman, A. (2012) *Applied Behavior Analysis for Teachers, 9th Edition*. Upper Saddle River, NJ: Pearson Education, Inc.

American Psychiatric Association (2013) *Diagnostic and Statistical Manual of Mental Disorders, 5th Edition*. Arlington, VA: American Psychiatric Publishing.

American Speech-Language-Hearing Association (1995) *Facilitated Communication Position Statement*. Available at www.asha.org/policy, accessed 25 May 2015.

Baron-Cohen, S. (1997) *Mindblindness: An Essay on Autism and Theory of Mind*. Cambridge, MA: A Bradford Book, MIT Press.

Beukelman, D. and Mirenda, P. (2012) *Augmentative and Alternative Communication: Supporting Children and Adults with Complex Communication Needs, Fourth Edition*. Baltimore, MD: Paul H. Brookes Publishing Co.

Caldwell, J. (2010) "What Is Good Reading and What Do Good Readers Do?" In C. Carnahan and P. Williamson (eds.) *Quality Literacy Instruction for Students with Autism Spectrum Disorder*. Shawnee Mission, KS: Autism Asperger Publishing Company.

Collucci, A. (2011) *Big Picture Thinking: Using Central Coherence Theory to Support Social Skills, A Book for Students*. Shawnee Mission, KS: Autism Asperger Publishing Company.

Common Core State Standards Initiative (2015) *Read the Standards*. Available at www.corestandards.org, accessed 28 August 2015.

Exkorn, K. (2005) *The ASD Sourcebook: Everything You Need to Know About Diagnosis, Treatment, Coping, and Healing*. New York, NY: Harper Collins.

Forest, E., Horner, R., Lewis-Palmer, T. and Todd, A. (2004) "Transitions for young children with autism from preschool to kindergarten." *Journal of Positive Behavior Interventions, 6*, 2, 13–112.

Ginsberg, M. (2012) "Invaluable allies: Partnering with parents for student success." *Educational Horizons, 90*, 3, 16–22.

Gottschall, J. (2012) *The Storytelling Animal: How Stories Make Us Human*. New York: Houghton Mifflin, Harcourt Publishing Company.

Grandin, T. and Panek, R. (2013) *The Autistic Brain: Thinking Across the Spectrum*. New York: Houghton Mifflin, Harcourt Publishing Company.

Gray, C. (2010) *The New Social Story Book, Revised and Expanded 10th Anniversary Edition: Over 150 Social Stories that Teach Everyday Social Skills to Children with Autism or Asperger's Syndrome and Their Peers*. Arlington, TX: Future Horizons.

Hala, S., Rasmussen, C. and Henderson, A. (2005) "Three types of source monitoring by children with and without autism: The role of executive function." *Journal of Autism and Developmental Disorders, 35,* 1, 75–89.

Happé, F. and Firth, U. (2006) "The weak coherence account: Detail-focused cognitive style in autism spectrum disorders." *Journal of Autism and Developmental Disorders, 36,* 1, 5–25.

Heward, W. (2006) *Exceptional Children: An Introduction to Special Education, 8th Edition.* Upper Saddle River, NJ: Pearson Education, Inc.

Hughes, A. and Read, V. (2012) *Building Positive Relationships with Parents of Young Children: A Guide to Effective Communication.* Florence, KY: Routledge, Taylor and Francis Group.

Kabot, S. and Reeve, C. (2010) *Setting Up Classroom Spaces that Support Students with Autism Spectrum Disorders.* Shawnee Mission, KS: Autism Asperger Publishing Company.

Kinder IQ website Available at www.kinderiq.com, accessed on 3 September 2015.

Lashno, M. (2010) *Mixed Signals: Understanding and Treating Your Child's Sensory Processing Issues.* Bethesda, MD: Woodbine House.

Moraine, P. (2012) *Helping Students Take Control of Everyday Executive Functions: The Attention Fix.* London: Jessica Kingsley Publishers.

Myles, B., Trautman, M. and Schelvan, R. (2004) *The Hidden Curriculum: Practical Solutions for Understanding Unstated Rules in Social Situations.* Shawnee Mission, KS: Autism Asperger Publishing Company.

Nichols, S. (2013) *Focus on Feelings: Teaching Emotion Understanding and Regulation.* Presented at Milestones Annual Autism Spectrum Disorder Conference, Cleveland, Ohio, June 19, 2013.

Rose, T. (2013) *Square Peg: My Story and What it Means for Raising Innovators, Visionaries, and Out-of-the-Box Thinkers.* New York: Hyperion.

Schetter, P. (2009) *Homeschooling the Child with Autism: Answers to the Top Questions Parents and Professionals Ask.* San Francisco, CA: Jossey-Bass.

Shaul, J. (2014) *The Conversation Train: A Visual Approach to Conversation for Children on the Autism Spectrum.* London: Jessica Kingsley Publishers.

Silva, L. and Schalock, M. (2012) "Autism Parenting Stress Index: Initial psychometric evidence." *Journal of Autism and Developmental Disorders, 42,* 4, 566–74.

Sinha, P., Kjelgaard, M., Gandhi, T., Tsourides, K. *et al.* (2014) "Autism as a disorder of prediction." *National Academy of Sciences (U.S.),* 2014–10. Available at http://hdl.handle.net/1721.1/90824, accessed on 1 July 2015.

Tanguay, P. (2001) *Nonverbal Learning Disabilities at Home: A Parent's Guide.* London: Jessica Kingsley Publishers.

Tantam, D. (2009) *Can the World Afford Autistic Spectrum Disorder? Nonverbal Communication, Asperger Syndrome, and the Interbrain.* London: Jessica Kingsley Publishers.

Teachtown website. Available at www.teachtown.com, accessed on 1 September 2015.

The Transporters website. Available at www.transporters.com, accessed on 3 September 2015.

U.S. Department of Education (2015) *Building the Legacy: IDEA 2004*. Available at http://idea.ed.gov, accessed 5 July 2015.

Wildenger, L. and McIntyre, L. (2011) "Family concerns and involvement during kindergarten." *Journal of Child and Family Studies, 20,* 387–396.

Williams, K. and Poel, E. (2006) "Stress management for special educators: The Self-Administered Tool for Awareness and Relaxation (STAR)." *Teaching Exceptional Children Plus, 3,* 1, 1–12.

Wong, C., Odom, S., Hume, K., Cox, A. *et al.* (2014) *Evidence-Based Practices for Children, Youth, and Young Adults with Autism Spectrum Disorder*. Chapel Hill, NC: Autism Evidence-Based Practice Review Group, Frank Porter Graham Child Development Institute, University of North Carolina at Chapel Hill. Available at http://fpg.unc.edu/sites/fpg.unc.edu/files/resources/reports-and-policy-briefs/2014-EBP-Report.pdf, accessed 25 May 2015.

Further Reading

Academics

Adkins, J. and Larkey, S. (2013) *Practical Mathematics for Children with an Autism Spectrum Disorder and Other Development Delays.* London: Jessica Kingsley Publishers.

Boucher, C. and Oehler, K. (2013) *I Hate to Write! Tips for Helping Students with Autism Spectrum and Related Disorders Increase Achievement, Meet Academic Standards, and Become Happy, Successful Writers.* Shawnee Mission, KS: Autism Asperger Publishing Company.

Henry, K. (2010) *How Do I Teach This Kid to Read? Teaching Literacy Skills to Young Children with Autism, from Phonics to Fluency.* Arlington, TX: Future Horizons.

Iland, E. (2011) *Drawing a Blank: Improving Comprehension for Readers on the Autism Spectrum.* Shawnee Mission, KS: Autism Asperger Publishing Company.

Kluth, P. and Danaher, S. (2010) *From Tutor Scripts to Talking Sticks: 100 Ways to Differentiate Instruction in K–12 Inclusive Classrooms.* Baltimore, MD: Brookes Publishing.

Kluth, P. and Danaher, S. (2013) *From Text Maps to Memory Caps: 100 More Ways to Differentiate Instruction in K–12 Inclusive Classrooms.* Baltimore, MD: Brookes Publishing.

Behavior

Baker, J. (2008) *No More Meltdowns: Positive Strategies for Managing and Preventing Out-of-Control Behavior.* Arlington, TX: Future Horizons, Inc.

Moyes, R. (2002) *Addressing the Challenging Behavior of Children with High-Functioning Autism/Asperger Syndrome in the Classroom: A Guide for Teachers and Parents.* London: Jessica Kingsley Publishers.

Richman, S. (2006) *Encouraging Appropriate Behavior for Children on the Autism Spectrum: Frequently Asked Questions.* London: Jessica Kingsley Publishers.

Cognitive theories

Collucci, A. (2010) *Big Picture Thinking: Using Central Coherence Theory to Support Social Skills.* Shawnee Mission, KS: Autism Asperger Publishing Company.

Gray, C. (2010) *The New Social Story Book, Revised and Expanded 10th Anniversary Edition: Over 150 Social Stories that Teach Everyday Social Skills to Children with Autism or Asperger's Syndrome and Their Peers.* Arlington, TX: Future Horizons.

Howlin, P., Baron-Cohen, S. and Hadwin, J. (1999) *Teaching Children with Autism to Mind-Read: A Practical Guide.* West Sussex: John Wiley and Sons, Ltd.

Moraine, P. (2012) *Helping Students Take Control of Everyday Executive Functions: The Attention Fix.* London: Jessica Kingsley Publishers.

Moyes, R. (2014) *Executive Function "Dysfunction": Strategies for Educators and Parents.* London: Jessica Kingsley Publishers.

Ordetx, K. (2014) *Teaching the Basics of Theory of Mind: A Complete Curriculum with Supporting Materials for Children with Autism Spectrum Disorder and Related Social Difficulties Ages Approximately 5 to 9 Years.* London: Jessica Kingsley Publishers.

Homeschooling

Schetter, P. (2009) *Homeschooling the Child with Autism: Answers to the Top Questions Parents and Professionals Ask.* San Francisco, CA: Jossey-Bass.

IEP

Lauer, V. (2013) *When the School Says No, How to Get to Yes! Securing Special Educations Services for Your Child.* London: Jessica Kingsley Publishers.

Wright, P. W., Wright, P. D. and O'Connor, S. (2010) *Wrightslaw: All About IEPs.* Hartfield, VA: Harbor House Law Press, Inc.

Sensory

Grandin, T. and Panek, R. (2013) *The Autistic Brain: Thinking Across the Spectrum.* New York: Houghton Mifflin Harcourt Publishing Company.

Kabot, S. and Reeve, C. (2010) *Setting Up Classroom Spaces that Support Students with Autism Spectrum Disorders.* Shawnee Mission, KS: Autism Asperger Publishing Company.

Koomar, J., Kranowitz, C. and Szklut, S. (2007) *Answers to Questions Teachers Ask About Sensory Integration: Forms, Checklists, and Practical Tools.* Arlington, TX: Future Horizons, Inc.

Rogers, L. (2013) *Visual Supports for Visual Thinkers: Practical Ideas for Students With Autism Spectrum Disorders and Other Special Education Needs.* London: Jessica Kingsley Publishers.

Reebye, P. and Stalker, A. (2008) *Understanding Regulation Disorders of Sensory Processing in Children.* London: Jessica Kingsley Publishers.

Yack, E., Aquilla, P. and Sutton, S. (2015) *Building Bridges Through Sensory Integration, 3rd Edition: Therapy for Children with Autism and Other Pervasive Developmental Disorders*. Arlington, TX: Future Horizons, Inc.

Social

Diamond, S. (2011) *Social Rules for Kids: The Top 100 Social Rules Kids Need to Succeed*. Shawnee Mission, KS: Autism Asperger Publishing Company.

Sher, B. (2009) *Early Intervention Games: Fun, Joyful Ways to Develop Social and Motor Skills in Children with Autism Spectrum or Sensory Processing Disorders*. San Francisco, CA: Jossey-Bass.

Helpful Websites

IDEA

The official website for IDEA:
idea.ed.gov

Kinder IQ

Free kindergarten readiness assessment is included with the website's learning program:
www.kinderiq.com/kindergarten-readiness-test.php

Understood

A supportive website for learning and attention issues:
www.understood.org

Wrightslaw

Focuses on special education law and advocacy:
www.wrightslaw.com

Index

of related interest

Parents Have the Power to Make Special Education Work
An Insider Guide
Judith Canty Graves and Carson Graves
Foreword by Robert K. Crabtree Esq.
ISBN 978 1 84905 970 1
eISBN 978 0 85700 878 7

101 Tips for Parents of Children with Autism
Effective Solutions for Everyday Challenges
Arnold Miller and Theresa C. Smith
Foreword by Paul J. Callahan
Afterword by Ethan B. Miller
ISBN 978 1 84905 960 2
eISBN 978 0 85700 818 3

Make Your Own Picture Stories for Kids with ASD (Autism Spectrum Disorder)
A DIY Guide for Parents and Carers
Brian Attwood
ISBN 978 1 84905 638 0
eISBN 978 1 78450 117 4

Autistic Logistics
A Parent's Guide to Tackling Bedtime, Toilet Training, Tantrums, Hitting, and Other Everyday Challenges
Kate Wilde
ISBN 978 1 84905 779 0
eISBN 978 1 78450 016 0